# THE TUSCARORA TRAIL

## A GUIDE TO THE

## NORTH HALF
### IN
### PENNSYLVANIA AND MARYLAND

1997
The Potomac Appalachian Trail Club
Vienna, Va

# THE TUSCARORA TRAIL
# A GUIDE TO THE NORTH HALF
in
Pennsylvania and Maryland

Written by
Thomas Lupp

## THIRD EDITION 1997

Cover Design by Michelle Curtin

L.C. No. 97-076060
ISBN 0-915746-80-8

Copyright © 1997
Potomac Appalachian Trail Club
Vienna, VA

Two roads diverged in a wood, and I-
I took the one less traveled by,
And that has made all the difference.

Robert Frost

Hikers and backpackers looking for a wilderness experience coupled with small towns, green pastures, and the crowing of roosters will find the Tuscarora Trail equal to, and in many ways superior to, the more famous and more traveled Appalachian Trail. This parallel trail forms a 250-mile mountaintop path to the west. It traverses an area that in many ways still resembles the quieter 19th century world that once prevailed.

# ACKNOWLEDGMENT

I would like to thank the people who assisted me with the completion of this guide: Mark Press, Ed Franco, Pete Brown, Rich Delaney, Christopher Firme, Richard Krabel, Laura Scudder, Lawrence Mushcamp, and David Keaton for collection of field data; Charlie Irvin, Jack Danner and all the maintainers and trail crews whose hard work saved and revitalized the trail; Elizabeth Johnston for encouraging me to write this edition of the trail guide. Also I would like to thank David Raphael for his work on the previous two editions of this guide.

Tom Lupp

# CONTENTS

Contents .................... v
Forward ..................... vii
The Tuscarora Trail ............... ix
Some History Along the Trail ......... xv
Summary of Distances (PA-MD) ........ xx
Sterrets Gap (Section 1) ............. 1
Flat Rock (Section 2) .............. 11
Blue Mountain (Section 3) ........... 21
Amberson Ridge (Section 4) .......... 27
Knob Mountain (Section 5) .......... 37
Cowans Gap (Section 6) ............ 47
Tuscarora Summit (Section 7) ........ 59
The Lockings (Section 8) ........... 67
Licking Creek (Section 9) ........... 77
C&O Canal (Section 10) ............ 85

Summary of Distances (PA-MD-WV-VA)
Inside back cover

# DISCLAIMER

Because of the constantly changing conditions due to natural and other causes beyond the control and/or knowledge of PATC, KTA and Tuscarora Trail maintainers, as well as the authors and contributors to this publication, PATC must disclaim any liability whatsoever for the condition of the trails, occurrences on it, or the accuracy of any data or material set forth in this trail guide. The trail guide was prepared on the basis of the best knowledge available to the authors at the time of publication. It must be presumed that all persons using this guide do so at their own risk.

*The purity of water from natural sources found along trails cannot be guaranteed. All water from natural sources should be treated before use.*

# FOREWORD

With the publishing of this third edition of the Tuscarora Trail guide several changes have taken place with the trail. The former Big Blue Trail is now officially part of the Tuscarora Trail, thus one name for this continuous long trail. The guide to the trail is published in two parts, being divided in Hancock, MD, at the C&O Canal towpath. Both guides are published by the Potomac Appalachian Trail Club. In the spring of 1997 the orange blazes in Pennsylvania and Maryland were replaced with blue blazes, giving continuity to the trail along its length.

The trail was remeasured in Pennsylvania and Maryland in 1996, and in Virginia and West Virginia in 1995 and 1996. Along with the new set of trail guides, new trail maps have been published to cover the trail route. As this guide goes to press, the directions, and conditions of the trail are accurate. However, a trail is a living thing and it will change with time. There are also relocations that will occur in the next few years to improve it.

If a stream or spring is labeled intermittent, do not expect to find water in dry weather, especially in late summer or fall. *The Potomac Appalachian Trail Club (PATC) is not responsible for the quality of water found along the trail. All water from natural sources should be purifed before use.* Many sections of the trail are dry; therefore, you are urged to carry adequate water.

Although a large portion of the Tuscarora Trail is on public land it also crosses privately owned land. Since you are a guest of the landowner, please show respect by staying on the trail and by not camping on private property. On valley roads hikers may encounter dogs which may or may not be friendly. A good hiking stick is your best defense. Since there are few shelters or established campgrounds along the trail, a small backpacker's stove and a tent are strongly advised for long-distance hikers. It is possible to travel for days on the Tuscarora Trail without meeting another hiker. Therefore, if you are planning a long hike, leave an itinerary with someone. For safety's sake do not hike in deer hunting season.

The northern half, the original Tuscarora Trail, was built by several member clubs and individuals of the Keystone Trails Association (KTA) while the southern half was built, as the Big Blue Trail, by the Potomac Appalachian Trail Club. The entire trail is now maintained by several chapters and individuals of PATC.

PATC is a volunteer organization which maintains the Tuscarora Trail and many other trails including a large section of the Appalachian Trail. The Club welcomes additional volunteer help for this purpose. To contact the Club write:

Potomac Appalachian Trail Club
118 Park Street, S.E.
Vienna, VA 22180
or call on weekday evenings: (703) 242-0315

KTA is an alliance of organizations and individuals who share a common interest in hiking opportunities in Pennsylvania and neighboring states. To contact the association write:

Keystone Trails Association
P.O. Box 251
Cogan Station, Pa 17728

# HISTORY

## The Tuscarora Trail

### Introduction

The Tuscarora Trail is an extensive bypass route of the Appalachian Trail in Pennsylvania, Maryland, West Virginia and Virginia. This route is approximately 250 miles long and connects the Appalachian Trail at both its northern and southern ends. This complete trail, known as the Tuscarora Trail, was originally built as separate trails, the Tuscarora Trail in the north and the Big Blue Trail in the south. The Tuscarora Trail departs to the west from the Appalachian Trail at the top of Blue Mountain about 10 miles west of the Susquehanna River and Harrisburg, PA. This occurs just before the Appalachian Trail descends south to make its crossing of the Cumberland Valley. It then proceeds on a general southwesterly direction, mostly on ridgetops. After following Blue Mountain the trail crosses Path Valley where it climbs the Tuscarora Mountain. At the end of the Tuscarora Mountain it descends, passes into Maryland where it follows the towpath of the C&O Canal to the town of Hancock. After crossing the Potomac River and following it downstream, the trail follows rural roads and climbs several small ridges, including Sleepy Creek

Mountain. It then descends into a campground before leaving West Virginia and starting a long valley crossing, mostly on roads, to Gore, VA. South of Gore the trail climbs and follows the crest of Great North Mountain and the valley to the west. The trail turns east, crosses Little North Mountain at Fetzer Gap, and descends into the Shenandoah Valley. After the valley crossing the trail crosses several ridges of the Massanutten Mountain before climbing the Blue Ridge Mountains of Shenandoah National Park and rejoining the Appalachian Trail. This junction is south of the Hogback Overlook at milepost 21 on the Skyline Drive.

## History of the Tuscarora Trail

In the early 1960s there was a real concern that the Appalachian Trail (AT) might become impossible to maintain due to the closing of the Trail by private land owners. To insure that a continuous footpath might be preserved, the Appalachian Trail Conference appointed committees to explore possible alternatives to part of the AT which appeared to be endangered. One of these areas was in northern Virginia between Shenandoah National Park and Harpers Ferry. The original committee for this bypass consisted of Lloyd Felton (Chmn.), Jim Denton (VA) and Martin Brillhart (PA). The bypass was to run from the Appalachian Trail in Deans Gap in Pennsylvania to a point in the Shenandoah National Park south of Front Royal, VA. The purpose was to create a route to the west, which would use public lands to the maximum in territory not yet afflicted with development and commercial pressure.

In the north a group from York, PA with Martin Brillhart laid out the route south to US 30, just south of Cowans Gap State Park. This was done with close cooperation of the Pennsylvania Bureau of Forestry and the Pennsylvania Game Commission. Once the location was established these departments were successful in acquiring some of the lands traversed which were not yet in public hands. From US 30 south to the Potomac River, Lloyd Felton completed the job of laying out the route. The actual building of the trail was supervised by Al McDonald with the help of several member clubs and individuals of the Keystone Trails Association. The first trail guide was published in 1979.

In the early to mid 80s tree mortality caused by gypsy moth defoliation led to a severe maintenance problem with vegetation growth. Although several long time maintainers continued to work on their sections, the overall condition of the trail was poor. There was even talk of abandoning the trail. In the early 90s the North Chapter of PATC, with Charlie Irvin as District Trails Manager, took on the job of reopening the trail. By 1995 the trail was reopened and the club was leading section hikes that covered the entire trail north of Hancock.

In the south, James W. Denton and A.J. (Woody) Kennedy were scouting the route for the then Big Blue Trail. From 1967 to 1972 Fred Blackburn spearheaded the planning and layout for the trail. He also supervised the construction of the southern section. By 1970 fifty-four miles of trail had been built and blazed, and six more miles were ready to be constructed. After Fred Blackburn's retirement in 1972, David Brownlie and

Howard Weise constructed an additional three miles of trail.

In 1974 Tom Floyd agreed to finish the last 66 miles of trail. Seventy percent of this was on private land. It was Floyd's job to find out who the landowners were, convince them to permit the trail to cross their land, and then supervise the building of the trail with volunteer labor. The trail was finally completed on October 11, 1981 in Lucas Woods near Great North Mountain, a short distance from the Virginia-West Virginia state line. Fred Blackburn, who was present when the first blaze was painted, was there to paint the last one. The first trail guide to the Big Blue Trail was published in 1984.

Gypsy moth defoliation also caused problems on the southern portion of the trail in the mid to late 80s. Keeping the trail clear of vegetation was a constant battle. In the 90s portions of the trail were used for PATC's Dogwood Half Hundred hike, which helped get much needed maintenance on a large portion of the trail.

In 1995, with the entire Tuscarora-Big Blue trail route open its entire length, PATC Council voted to drop the Big Blue Trail name and call the entire trail the Tuscarora Trail. It was also agreed that the northern portion would be reblazed in blue. KTA Council and Pennsylvania Bureau of Forestry also voted and agreed on these changes. Changing of signs and blazes was completed in 1997.

*Trail sign at PA 233*

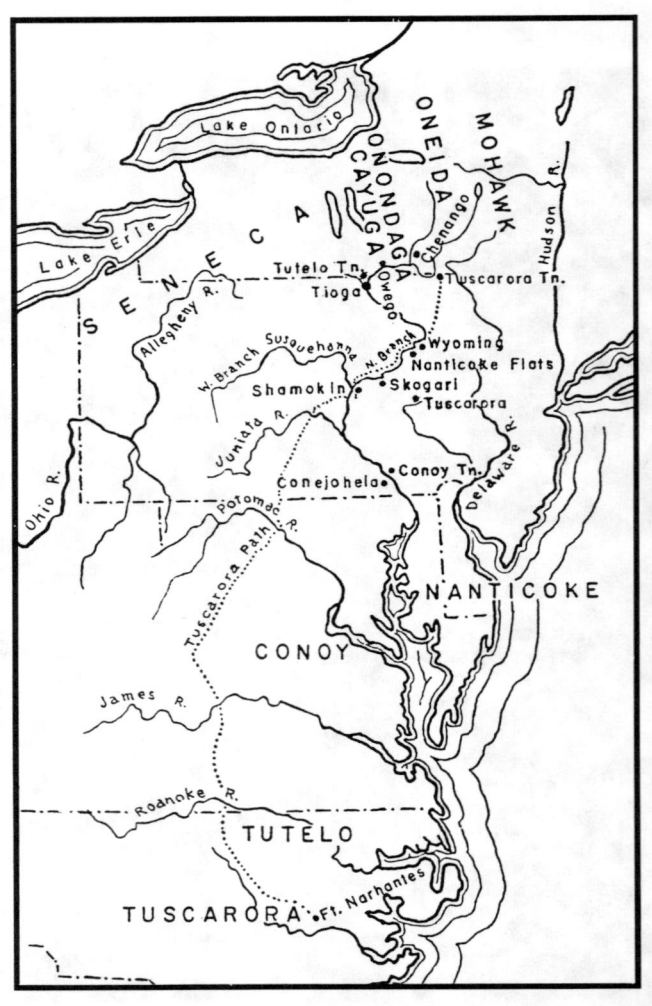

*Movement of Refugee Peoples to the Iroquois Country from* Indians in Pennsylvania; see page xv.

# Some History Along the Trail

## The Tuscarora Indians

"from *Indians in Pennsylvania* by Paul A.W. Wallace, published by the Pennsylvania Historical and Museum Commission, and used with their permission."

The name Tuscarora is a corruption of Skaru-ren, "hemp gatherers." The Tuscarora Indians were an Iroquoian people whose homes originally were in North Carolina on streams flowing east into Pamlico Sound. John Lawson, an early explorer and historian, knew them intimately and described them as mild and friendly. But, it was a recognized business among white men of those days to kidnap Tuscarora children and sell them as slaves, so the Indians at length turned savagely on the whites and massacred them indiscriminately. John Lawson himself was captured in 1711 and put to death. The Tuscarora War which followed was not ended until 1713, when the last great Tuscarora fort, Narhantes, near Snow Hill in Green County, North Carolina, was destroyed.

Some Tuscarora families headed north at once for the country of the Five Nations, with whom the Tuscaroras had been in touch by way of what the Iroquois called the Tuscarora Path. In 1714 the chiefs of the Five Nations informed Governor Robert Hunter at Albany that the "Tuscarore Indians are come to shelter themselves among the Five Nations…they were of us and went from us long ago and are now returned…we desire you to look upon the Tuscarores that are come to live among us as our children who shall obey our commands and live peaceably and orderly." After the adoption of the Tuscaroras, the Five Nations became known as the Six Nations.

It was ninety years before the migration of the Tuscaroras from North Carolina to the Iroquois country was completed. They moved in bands at different times, at different rates of speed, and by different routes. They stopped "overnight" at points along the way. That is why their passage through Pennsylvania is marked by so many place names: Path Valley, after the Tuscarora Path and Tuscarora Creek in Huntingdon and Juniata Counties; another Tuscarora Creek in Wyoming County, a Tuscarora Post Office in Schuylkill County, and a village by that name in Juniata County; Tuscarora Mountain west of the Kittatiny; and Tuscarora Old Town, shown on early maps at the Great Bend in Susquehanna County. As can be seen, the Tuscarora Trail passes through the region of this migration and uses several of these locations.

Early documents show that the Iroquois not only encouraged but actively superintended this migration. In 1765 they dispatched several Tuscaroras south to bring away the last remnant of their people in North Carolina. These latter had sold their lands and with part of the proceeds bought horses for the long journey north. Setting out the next spring, 160 or more of them under the guidance of two chiefs and an interpreter, moved unmolested over what were now the white man's roads until they reached Harris' Ferry (now Harrisburg). There the Paxton Boys (who had murdered the Indians at Conestoga in 1763) were still operating. The Tuscaroras were plundered, losing among other things, six horses. At Lackawanna (Pittston) the travelers divided into two parties, one going directly north to Tuscarora Town by the Lackawanna Path, while the other took a longer but easier route over the Great Warriors Path, which followed the Susquehanna River.

They had sent messengers ahead, in accordance with Indian custom, to let the Iroquois know at what time to expect them. The Iroquois not only made preparations to receive them but also sent agents to arrange for their comfort along the way. After the robberies at Harris' Ferry, it was necessary to provide transportation for their sick and aged. The emissaries of the Six Nations, Newallike and Aehkolunty along with others in five canoes, left a request among "the Indians everywhere along the Susquehanna" as the Moravian missionary at Wyalusing, John Jacob Schmick, noted on November 18, 1766, "to receive these poor Indians, send canoes from place to place for them and provide them with corn so that they may get along all right. Our Indians, accordingly, as soon as they hear of their arrival at Lechawachneck (Pittston) will send 10 canoes to them."

The Tuscaroras were admitted to the Longhouse, Council of the Five Nations, under the sponsorship of one of the original Five Nations. At first they were proteges of the Oneidas, later of the Senecas. The Tuscarora are still in the Seneca country on a reservation near Lewiston at the mouth of the Niagara Gorge. A population of about 600 is headquartered at Tuscarora

Rural Community, Niagara County, New York, about nine miles northeast of Niagara Falls.

## The Tuscarora Path

The Tuscarora Path was the route used by the Tuscarora Indians to find refuge in the Iroquois country of northern Pennsylvania and upstate New York. On their way north, Tuscarora bands scattered widely in Pennsylvania and stayed for considerable periods at places they liked, as the name "Tuscarora" on hills and creeks attests.

From their homelands in the coastal plain of North Carolina they followed the Tuscarora Path northwest to Virgina. The path crossed the Roanoke (Staunton) River just north of the state border. Traveling across the Piedmont of Virginia they crossed the James River northeast of Lynchburg. Crossing the Blue Ridge west of Charlottesville, the path turned north in the Shenandoah Valley just south of Staunton. The path then came up the Shenandoah Valley past Staunton, Woodstock, Winchester and Martinsburg to cross the Potomac at Cherry Run. Once inside Pennsylvania, the Tuscarora Path ran north to Mercersburg and the present town at Fort Loudon, there entering what is now known as Path Valley. Passing Richmond Furnace, the Tuscarora Path continued up the valley of the West Branch Conococheague Creek through Fannettsburg, Springtown, Willow Hill, Spring Run and Dry Run. At Concord Narrows it passed north through the gap in Tuscarora Mountain and bending eastward, ran along the east bank of Tuscarora Creek to East Waterford.

Continuing northeast, it left for a time the winding creek and took a straight course past Honey Grove, Reed's School and Path. It touched00 the Tuscarora Creek again at Seven Pines and went to cross the Juniata River at Port Royal, the ford being just below the mouth of Tuscarora Creek. Continuing northeastward past the present day towns of McAlisterville, Bunkertown, Swales, Richfield and Freeburg, the Tuscarora Path reached the Susquehanna at Selinsgrove. Crossing Penn's Creek it forded the Susquehanna to the Indian town of Shamokin (Sunbury).

From this point, the Tuscarora probably followed the North Branch of the Susquehanna to Wyoming (Wilkes-Barre). From Wilkes-Barre and Pittston, some bands took the Lackawanna Path directly to Apple Tree Town at Great Bend, while others took the canoe route (with its accompanying path) up the North Branch Valley past Tunkhannock, Wyalusing, Tioga (Athens) and Owego.

The Tuscarora Trail of today should not be construed as following the path of the Indians who generally traveled in the valleys and along streams, crossing the mountains at a pass or gap. The trail does touch the route of the Indians where the trail crosses The Shenandoah Valley in Virgina and at Path Valley near the village of Spring Run in Pennsylvania. In general, it follows ridgetops above the valleys used by the Tuscaroras in their travels northward.

## SUMMARY OF DISTANCES

|  | N to S miles | N to S cum. mi. | S to N cum. mi. |
|---|---|---|---|
| Appalachian Trail | 0.0 | 0.0 | 109.8 |
| PA 34 | 2.5 | 2.5 | 107.3 |
| PA 74 | 10.0 | 12.5 | 97.3 |
| Colonel Denning S.P.(PA 233) | 12.4 | 24.9 | 84.9 |
| Cowpens Road | 8.6 | 33.5 | 76.3 |
| Hemlock Road | 8.8 | 42.3 | 67.5 |
| PA 641 | 11.6 | 53.9 | 55.9 |
| Cowans Gap S.P. | 15.8 | 69.7 | 40.1 |
| US 30 | 6.8 | 76.5 | 33.3 |
| PA 16 | 1.9 | 78.4 | 31.4 |
| PA 456 | 14.5 | 92.9 | 16.9 |
| C&O Canal | 9.0 | 101.9 | 7.9 |
| Hancock, MD | 7.9 | 109.8 | 0.0 |

# Section 1

# STERRETS GAP

Appalachian Trail to PA 74
Distance 12.5 miles

**Brief Description of the Section**

The Sterrets Gap section begins at the junction of the Tuscarora, Darlington and Appalachian trails on Blue Mountain in State Game Lands #170 (elev. 1260 ft). Camping is not permitted in PA State Game Lands. The trail descends slightly into Deans Gap, the former terminus of the trail, continues along Blue Mountain and then descends into Sterrets Gap at PA 34 (elev. 932 ft). Sterrets Gap has a long history of use. In the 1700s it was a major trade route with the Indians to the west. During the War of 1812 U.S. Army Dispatch Riders passed through the gap on the way to the Canadian Border. Confederate soldiers advanced to within one and a quarter miles of the gap on June 27, 1863, four days before the Battle of Gettysburg. At that time Perry Countians swarmed to the mountain pass, hastily fortified it, and awaited the Confederates. From Sterrets Gap the trail descends a short distance along PA 34 then reascends to the top of Blue Mountain. In Cranes Gap (elev. 1240 ft) the trail intersects a cross mountain road to Carlisle, built in 1772. The trail continues along the ridge then descends the north side on Longs Gap Road. The trail passes the boundary of the Florence Jones Reineman Wildlife Sanctuary, established in 1966 as a sanctuary for all forms of wildlife. It is a Registered Natural Landmark and visitors are not permitted in the sanctuary. At the base of the ridge (elev. 900 ft) the trail turns and follows Polecat Road to PA 74 and Greens Valley Road.

**Parking**

1. There is no useable road access to the northern terminus of the Tuscarora Trail at its junction with the Appalachian Trail. Access by foot only.
   A. From the east the Darlington Trail goes on Blue Mountain from US 11 and US 15 on the west side of the Susquehanna River at Overview to the junction in 10.7 mi.
   B. From the north the Appalachian Trail climbs Blue Mountain 2.1 mi from its junction with PA 850, west of the village of Keystone, approximately 9 mi west of Marysville. There are two Game Commission parking areas here. One is located 0.4 mi north of the highway at the end of the gravel road which the trail utilizes. This parking area may be closed to the public at certain times of the year. The other is located 0.4 mi east of the gravel road on the south side of PA 850.
   C. From the south the Appalachian Trail climbs Blue Mountain 1.8 mi from its junction with PA 944. Very limited parking along PA 944. There

are other possible parking areas along the Appalachian Trail south of PA 944.

2. From the Appalachian Trail crossing on PA 850, continue west on PA 850 to Grier Point, approximately 10 mi west of Marysville. Take Mountain Road south for 1.2 mi to a Game Commission parking lot on the left, where the road bears hard right in Myers Gap. From the parking lot, follow the jeep road 1.2 mi to Deans Gap. Mountain Road continues southwest to Sterrets Gap.

3. Trail crosses PA 34 in Sterrets Gap 7 mi north of Carlisle. Day use parking available, with permission, at used car lot in gap. Call Richard & Associates, Inc. at (717) 241-5884 for permission.

4. At south end of section, junction of PA 74 and Greens Valley Road approximately 3.0 mi south of Bridgeport. Parking, with permission, available at Milt's Garage & Body Shop, R.D. 1, Landisburg, PA. Also 0.6 mi west on Greens Valley Road. Where the trail turns right(north) onto gravel drive, there is limited parking on right side of lane.

## Maps

PATC Map J
USGS 7½' Quadrangles: Wertzville, Pa.; Shermans Dale, Pa.; Landisburg, Pa.

## Useful Information

**Emergency-**Dial 911

**Services**-Carlisle has post office, restaurants and stores. Carlisle Springs 3.0 mile south of Sterretts Gap has P.O., Hunters Inn, bar/restaurant, located approximately 1 mi north of Sterrets Gap on PA 34.

## SECTION 1
## NORTH TO SOUTH

Detailed Trail Data

Miles

0.0   Northern terminus of Tuscarora Trail at its junction with Appalachian Trail and Darlington Trail. Follow Tuscarora Trail west along Blue Mountain ridgetop on jeep road, passing through State Game Lands #170, with game lands on both sides. (Appalachian Trail to right,north, leads 0.1 mi to Darlington Shelter and a *spring*. Darlington Trail continues east along Blue Mountain for 10.7 mi to Overview and the Susquehanna River.)

0.7   Deans Gap, former terminus of Tuscarora Trail. (The cross mountain road in gap is former route of Appalachian Trail. Road to right,northwest, passable by four-wheel drive leads to Mountain Road and parking in Myers Gap in 1.2 mi.) Continue ahead on jeep road.

1.7   Boundary of State Game Lands #170. Leave game lands.

2.2   Arrive at double powerlines. Extensive view to right(north). Continue west and descend ridgetop.

| | |
|---|---|
| 2.45 | Turn left onto Mountain Road just south of paved driveway. |
| 2.5 | Junction of PA 34 and Mountain Road in Sterretts Gap. Turn right(northwest) onto PA 34 and descend ridge along road. Pass used car lot on left. |
| 3.1 | Turn left(southwest) off PA 34 onto private driveway. Continue ahead on driveway. |
| 3.2 | Pass house on right. Enter woods and continue ahead on woods road. |
| 3.3 | Cross pipeline right-of-way. Continue ahead on woods road. |
| 3.6 | Cross stream. |
| 4.1 | Pass house and old trailer to right of road. |
| 4.2 | Pass through small clearing. Road comes in from right. Continue ahead on woods road and soon leave woods into powerline clearing. |
| 4.25 | Turn left(south) onto powerline jeep road and ascend steeply. |
| 4.6 | Turn right off powerline jeep road a short distance below ridgetop. Enter woods on trail. |
| 4.8 | View, to left looking south over Cumberland Valley. |
| 5.0 | Woods road comes in on right. Continue ahead on woods road. |
| 5.6 | Woods road comes in on right. |
| 5.8 | Boundary of State Game Lands #230. Enter game lands on both sides of trail. |
| 5.9 | Boundary of State Game Lands #230. Leave game lands. |
| 6.1 | Boundary of State Game Lands #230. Reenter game lands on both sides of trail. |

| | |
|---|---|
| 6.5 | Turn left(west) onto another woods road. (To right(north) blue-blazed road continues downhill to Fox Hollow Road.) |
| 6.6 | Cranes Gap; continue straight on woods road. (Road to left, south, was built in 1772 as a cross mountain road from Carlisle. It is 1.9 mi south to PA 944.) |
| 7.2 | Boundary of State Game Lands #230. Leave game lands. |
| 7.7 | Leave old woods road and ascend ridge on trail. |
| 8.5 | Cross old mountain road in gap. Continue along side of ridge. |
| 8.9 | Turn left onto road and begin to ascend ridge. |
| 9.1 | Level out and continue along north side of ridge. |
| 9.2 | Trail register; please sign in. Turn right onto Longs Gap Road and begin descent of Blue Mountain. (Longs Gap Road continues uphill and then descends south side of ridge into Carlisle. Spectacular view of Cumberland Valley at first switchback over crest of ridge.) |
| 9.7 | Join and follow boundary of F.J. Reineman Wildlife Sanctuary. **No Trespassing** in sanctuary. Keep on road. Continue descent. |
| 9.8 | Stream crosses road. |
| 9.9 | Bear left and leave boundary of sanctuary. |
| 10.0 | Woods road comes in from left. |
| 10.3 | Polecat Road. Turn left(west) and follow road. |
| 10.8 | Pass farm pond on right. |
| 11.9 | Bear right on Polecat Road at intersection. Cross stream. |
| 12.45 | PA 74. Turn left(southwest) on PA 74 and cross stream to Greens Valley Road. |

12.5 Junction of PA 74 and Greens Valley Road. End of Section 1. Trail turns right(west) on Greens Valley Road and passes garage on right.

## SECTION 1
## SOUTH TO NORTH

Miles  Detailed Trail Data
0.0  Junction of PA 74 and Greens Valley Road. Turn left(northwest) on PA 74 and cross stream to Polecat Road. Pass garage on left.
0.05  Polecat Road. Turn right(east) and follow Polecat Road.
0.6  Cross stream and bear left at intersection, on Polecat Road.
1.7  Pass farm pond on left.
2.2  Turn right(south) onto Longs Gap Road (woods road), leaving Polecat Road which bears left. Begin ascent of Blue Mountain.
2.5  Woods road comes in from right.
2.6  Bear right and follow boundary of F.J. Reineman Wildlife Sanctuary. **No Trespassing** in sanctuary. Keep on road and continue ascent.
2.7  Stream crosses road.
2.8  Leave boundary of sanctuary. Continue ascent.
3.3  Trail register; please sign in. Turn left off Longs Gap Road and continue along ridge on another woods road. (Longs Gap Road continues uphill and then descends south side of ridge into Carlisle. Spectacular view of Cumberland Valley at first switchback over crest of ridge.)

| | |
|---|---|
| 3.4 | Descend north side of ridge. |
| 3.6 | Turn right off road and begin to ascend ridge. |
| 4.0 | Cross old mountain road in gap. Proceed to climb on and off ridge several times over next 4 mi. |
| 4.8 | Descend from ridge and soon join old woods road which trail follows for next several miles. |
| 5.3 | Boundary of State Game Lands #230. Enter game lands on both sides of trail. |
| 5.9 | Cranes Gap; continue straight on woods road. (Road to right, south, was built in 1772 as a cross mountain road from Carlisle. It is 1.9 mi south to PA 944.) |
| 6.0 | Turn right(east) onto another woods road. Road, now blue-blazed, continues left(north) downhill to Fox Hollow Road. |
| 6.4 | Boundary of State Game Lands #230. Leave game lands. |
| 6.6 | Boundary of State Game Lands #230. Reenter game lands on both sides of trail. |
| 6.7 | Boundary of State Game Lands #230. Leave game lands. |
| 6.9 | Woods road comes in on left. |
| 7.5 | Woods road turns left. Continue ahead on ridge. |
| 7.7 | View to right, looking south over Cumberland Valley. Jog left off ridgetop to small saddle. |
| 7.9 | Powerline a short distance below ridgetop on north side. Turn left(south) on powerline jeep road and descend steeply. |
| 8.25 | Turn right(east) onto dirt road and enter woods. |
| 8.3 | Pass through small clearing. Road comes in from left. Continue ahead on woods road. |

| | |
|---|---|
| 8.4 | Pass house and old trailer to left of road. |
| 8.9 | Cross stream. |
| 9.2 | Cross pipeline right-of-way. Continue ahead on woods road. |
| 9.3 | Pass house on left. Continue on driveway. |
| 9.4 | PA 34. Turn right(southeast) and ascend ridge along road. |
| 10.0 | Junction of PA 34 and Mountain Road in Sterretts Gap. Turn left(northeast) onto Mountain Road. Pass used car lot on right. |
| 10.05 | Turn right(east) off Mountain Road into woods just before paved driveway and soon join a jeep road. |
| 10.3 | Double powerlines with extensive view to left(north). Continue east along Blue Mountain ridgetop on jeep road. |
| 10.8 | Boundary of State Game Lands #170. Enter game lands on both sides of trail. |
| 11.8 | Deans Gap, former terminus of Tuscarora Trail. (Cross mountain road in gap is former route of Appalachian Trail. Road to left, northwest, passable by four-wheel drive leads to Mountain Road and parking in Myers Gap in 1.2 mi.) Continue ahead on jeep road. |
| 12.5 | Northern terminus of Tuscarora Trail at its junction with Appalachian Trail and Darlington Trail. End of Section 1. Appalachian Trail to left(north) leads 0.1 mi to Darlington Shelter and a *spring*. Darlington Trail continues east along Blue Mountain for 10.7 mi to Overview at Susquehanna River. |

*View from Flat Rock*

# Section 2

# FLAT ROCK

PA 74 to Colonel Denning State Park (PA 233)
Distance 12.4 miles

**Brief Description of the Section**

This section is named for the large rock outcrop located near the southern end of the section in the Tuscarora State Forest. This section begins at the junction of PA 74 and Greens Valley Road. After traveling a short distance on Greens Valley Road the trail turns and climbs to the top of Barkley Ridge (elev. 1855 ft). This is a rise of approximately 1300 ft over a distance of about 3.2 mi. The trail then descends into McClures Gap, reclimbs the ridge and continues on Blue Mountain to Berrys Gap. The 2.7 mi from McClures Gap to Berrys Gap is one of the rockiest sections of the Tuscarora. From Berrys Gap the trail descends into Wildcat Hollow and enters the Tuscarora State Forest. The trail reascends Blue Mountain (elev. 1987 ft) to reach the Flat Rock Vista with spectacular views of the Cumberland Valley. Following the Flat Rock Trail the trail reaches the "Wagonwheel" trail junction at the top of the ridge above Doubling Gap. This gap is so named because Blue Mountain doubles on itself forming a deep reverse "S" shape before continuing southwest. The trail then descends into Doubling Gap and enters Colonel Denning State Park ending at PA 233.

For information on the Tuscarora State Forest or to obtain a public use map contact the forest at the following address:

Tuscarora State Forest
R.D. 1, Box 42-A
Blain, PA 17006
(717) 536-3191

For information on Colonel Denning State Park or to obtain a Park Recreation Guide contact the park at the following address:

Colonel Denning State Park
1599 Doubling Gap Road
Newville, PA 17241
(717) 776-5272

**Parking**

1. At north end of section, junction of PA 74 and Greens Valley Road approximately 3.0 mi south of Bridgeport. Parking with permission, available at Milt's Garage & Body Shop, R.D. 1, Landisburg, PA. Also 0.6 mi west on Greens Valley Road. Where the trail turns right(north) onto gravel drive there is limited parking on right side of lane.

2. At south end of section, along PA 233, 0.7 mi south of Colonel Denning State Park there is a hiker parking lot on Elk Hill Road. There is parking for about 10 cars.

There is no direct intermediate vehicle road access in this section. There is foot access on jeep roads to McClures Gap and Berrys Gap and access on several trails from the state park.

## Maps

PATC Map J
USGS 7½' Quadrangles: Landisburg, Pa.;
   Andersonburg, Pa.

## Useful Information

**Emergency**-Dial 911
**Services**-Colonel Denning State Park 0.7 mi north on PA 233. Pay phone at Park Office. Park facilities: Camping, swimming, fishing, nature center and food concession (all seasonal).


# SECTION 2
# NORTH TO SOUTH

| Miles | Detailed Trail Data |
|---|---|
| 0.0 | Junction of Greens Valley Road and PA 74. Turn right(west) and proceed on Greens Valley Road. Garage at this junction. |
| 0.6 | Pass entrance road to R.F. Reineman Wildlife Sanctuary Field Station on left. Turn right onto gravel driveway. |
| 0.7 | Turn left off gravel driveway near fork in road. Enter brushy woods on trail. |

| | |
|---|---|
| 0.8 | Cross corner of lawn passing house trailer on right. Cross farm road and enter woods. |
| 1.0 | At farm road turn left for 200 ft, then at intersection of farm roads turn left onto trail in woods. |
| 1.2 | Turn left then right on old logging road. |
| 1.3 | Ascend side hill trail above stream on left. |
| 1.4 | Turn right onto woods road. Ascend gently on road by stream. |
| 1.5 | Cascade to left of trail. |
| 1.6 | Pass logging road coming in on right then come to small cleared area. |
| 1.8 | *Spring* in draw to left of trail. |
| 1.9 | Bear left on road. Continue ascent. |
| 2.0 | Turn left onto another road in gap between Barkley Ridge and Welsh Hill. Ascend Barkley Ridge on road. |
| 2.3 | Woods road bears left. Continue ascent on trail. |
| 3.2 | Top of Barkley Ridge. Turn right onto road. (To left road enters R.F. Reineman Wildlife Sanctuary.) Descend steeply on road. |
| 3.5 | Cross jeep road in McClures Gap. (To left it is 1.6 mi down to a road passable by car to PA 944. To right jeep road descends into Kennedy Valley and a paved road leading to PA 74.) Go straight ahead past modern hunting cabin and reascend ridge. Follow narrow ridgetop for next 2.7 mi to Berrys Gap. (Trail is very rocky in some places and can be strenuous. Use caution in wet weather. Many dead trees apparent along Blue Mountain caused by gypsy moth defoliation in early 80s.) |

| | |
|---|---|
| 3.7 | Cross ridge, then turn left onto logging road. |
| 3.8 | Pass property-corner rock cairn to right of trail. Logging road ends. |
| 4.8 | Logging road drops down left side of ridge. |
| 4.9 | View to left(southeast) of Cumberland Valley. Trail register; please sign in. |
| 6.2 | Berrys Gap. Turn right onto woods road and descend from gap. (To left road continues down southeast side of Blue Mountain.) |
| 6.3 | Pass logging road on right. |
| 6.7 | Pass yellow-blazed logging road on right. This road descends into Kennedy Valley. |
| 7.3 | After crossing clearing at top of hill pass through a selective logging cut. Cross Tuscarora State Forest boundary and enter state forest at trail sign. |
| 7.5 | Junction with red-blazed Warner Trail on right. (Warner Trail leads 2.5 mi to the "Wagonwheel" trail junction via Trout Run in Kennedy Valley.) |
| 7.6 | Cross state forest boundary, leaving state forest. |
| 7.7 | White, rock-cairn corner marker of Tuscarora State Forest to left of trail. Cross boundary and reenter state forest. |
| 8.1 | *Spring* to left of trail. |
| 8.6 | Turn toward Wildcat Run in Wildcat Hollow. Neat campsite on far side of stream in hemlocks. |
| 9.2 | Junction with Lehman Trail on right. (Lehman Trail leads 0.5 mi north to "Wagonwheel" trail junction.) Continue up Wildcat Hollow. |
| 9.3 | Turn left and ascend out of Wildcat Hollow. |
| 9.9 | Cross top of Blue Mountain then turn right along east side of ridge. |

| | |
|---|---|
| 10.15 | Flat Rock Vista. Spectacular view of Cumberland Valley to southeast. Turn right(north) and follow Flat Rock Trail. |
| 10.2 | Top of ridge. Pass U.S. Geological Survey marker in rock in center of trail. |
| 10.8 | Cross headwaters of Wildcat Run. Possible campsite on north side of stream. |
| 11.2 | Top of ridge; arrive at "Wagonwheel" trail junction. Turn left onto a jeep road (Ickes Road) and descend ridge. (Straight ahead Flat Rock Trail leads 0.9 mi to Colonel Denning State Park. To right Warner Trail leads 2.5 mi to rejoin Tuscarora Trail via Kennedy Valley. Lehman Trail also goes right for 0.5 mi to rejoin Tuscarora Trail in Wildcat Hollow.) In 150 ft Woodburn Trail goes left(south) 1.6 mi to PA 233. |
| 11.5 | *Spring* to left of trail at switchback. |
| 12.0 | Tuscarora State Forest boundary. Leave state forest and enter private property of Doubling Gap Center. |
| 12.3 | Colonel Denning State Park boundary. Enter small section of state park. |
| 12.35 | Pass vehicle gate and woods road on right. Leave state park and turn right(north) onto PA 233. Enter Tuscarora State Forest. |
| 12.4 | Intersection of Elk Hill Road and PA 233. End of Section 2. Parking available at hiker parking lot on Elk Hill Road. Trail proceeds west on Elk Hill Road. |

# SECTION 2
# SOUTH TO NORTH

| Miles | Detailed Trail Data |
|---|---|
| 0.0 | Intersection of Elk Hill Road and PA 233, in Tuscarora State Forest. Parking available at hiker parking lot on Elk Hill Road. Proceed south on PA 233 to Ickes Road. |
| 0.05 | Turn left(east) onto jeep road (Ickes Road). Pass vehicle gate and woods road on left, leaving state forest. Enter small section of Colonel Denning State Park. Climb to top of ridge on Ickes Road. |
| 0.1 | State park boundary. Leave state park and enter private property of Doubling Gap Center. |
| 0.4 | Tuscarora State Forest boundary. Enter state forest and continue ascent. |
| 0.9 | *Spring* to right of trail at switchback. |
| 1.2 | Top of ridge. Woodburn Trail goes right(south) 1.6 mi to PA 233. In 150 ft reach "Wagonwheel" trail junction. Turn right and follow Flat Rock Trail. (To left Flat Rock Trail leads 0.9 mi to Colonel Denning State Park. Also to left Warner Trail leads 2.5 mi to rejoin Tuscarora Trail via Kennedy Valley. Lehman Trail goes straight ahead for 0.5 mi to rejoin Tuscarora Trail in Wildcat Hollow.) |
| 1.6 | Cross headwaters of Wildcat Run. Possible campsite on north side of stream. |
| 2.2 | Top of Blue Mountain. Pass U.S. Geological Survey marker in rock in center of trail. |

| | |
|---|---|
| 2.25 | Flat Rock Vista. Spectacular view of Cumberland Valley to southeast. Turn sharp left along east side of ridge. |
| 2.5 | Cross top of ridge, then descend into Wildcat Hollow. |
| 3.1 | Wildcat Run in Wildcat Hollow. Turn right and follow stream down hollow. |
| 3.2 | Junction with Lehman Trail on left. (Lehman Trail leads 0.5 mi north to "Wagonwheel" trail junction.) Continue down Wildcat Hollow. |
| 3.8 | Neat campsite on far side of stream in hemlocks. Trail soon turns away from stream. |
| 4.3 | *Spring* to right of trail. |
| 4.7 | White, rock-cairn corner marker of Tuscarora State Forest to right of trail. Cross boundary and leave state forest. |
| 4.8 | Cross state forest boundary and reenter state forest. |
| 4.9 | Junction with red-blazed Warner Trail on left. (Warner Trail leads 2.5 mi back to "Wagonwheel" trail junction via Trout Run in Kennedy Valley.) |
| 5.1 | Cross Tuscarora State Forest boundary and leave state forest at trail sign. After passing through selective logging cut, cross clearing at top of hill. Descend on woods road. |
| 5.7 | Pass yellow-blazed logging road on left. (Road descends into Kennedy Valley.) |
| 6.1 | Pass logging road on left and ascend to Berrys Gap. |
| 6.2 | Berrys Gap. Turn left off road which continues down southeast side of Blue Mountain. Follow |

|      | narrow ridgetop for next 2.7 mi to McClures Gap. (Trail is very rocky in some places and can be strenuous. Use caution in wet weather. Many dead trees apparent along Blue Mountain caused by gypsy moth defoliation in the early 80s.) |
|------|---|
| 7.5  | View to right (southeast) of Cumberland Valley. Trail register; please sign in. |
| 7.6  | Logging road drops down right side of ridge. |
| 8.6  | Pass property-corner rock cairn to left of trail. Meet and follow logging road, becoming less rocky. |
| 8.7  | Turn right off logging road. Cross ridge and continue on south side of ridge. |
| 8.9  | Pass modern hunting cabin and arrive at jeep road in McClures Gap. (To right it is 1.6 mi down to a road passable by car to PA 944. To left jeep road descends into Kennedy Valley and a paved road leading to PA 74.) Continue ahead on road ascending steeply. |
| 9.2  | Top of Barkley Ridge. Turn left off of road that enters R.F. Reineman Wildlife Sanctuary. Descend gradually. |
| 10.1 | Join woods road which comes in on right. Continue descent on road. |
| 10.4 | Turn right on road that passes through gap between Barkley Ridge and Welsh Hill. |
| 10.5 | Turn right on road going downhill. |
| 10.6 | *Spring* in draw to right of trail. |
| 10.8 | Come to small cleared area with stream to right. Pass logging road going left and continue descent on road by stream. |
| 10.9 | Cascade to right of trail. |

| | |
|---|---|
| 11.0 | Turn left off road onto side hill trail above stream. |
| 11.2 | Turn left then right on old logging road. |
| 11.4 | At intersection of farm roads, turn right for 200 ft then bear right onto trail in woods. |
| 11.6 | Farm road at edge of lawn. Cross corner of lawn passing house trailer on left. Enter brushy woods. |
| 11.7 | Exit woods and turn right onto gravel driveway near fork in road. Continue ahead on driveway. |
| 11.8 | Turn left off gravel driveway onto paved Greens Valley Road. Pass entrance road to R.F. Reineman Wildlife Sanctuary Field Station on right at stone bridge. |
| 12.4 | Junction of Greens Valley Road and PA 74. End of Section 2. Trail turns left(north) and proceeds a short distance on PA 74 to Polecat Road. Garage at this junction. |

# Section 3

# BLUE MOUNTAIN

Colonel Denning State Park (PA 233) to Cowpens Road
Distance 8.6 miles

**Brief Description of Section**

This section is almost entirely in the Tuscarora State Forest as it follows the crest of Blue Mountain. The trail leaves PA 233 on Elk Hill Road and soon follows several old woods roads to ascend to the top of Blue Mountain ridge (elev. 1690 ft). This is a rise of approximately 1000 ft over a distance of 1.3 mi. The trail then descends to the north and reclimbs the ridge to a very rough and rocky ridgetop, gradually ascending to an elevation exceeding 2000 ft over a distance of about 6.0 mi. After a short descent it continues on a level course paralleling Cowpens Road until it reaches Old Ramp Trail which it follows to Cowpens Road. See Section 2 for information on the Tuscarora State Forest and Colonel Denning State Park.

**Parking**

1. At north end of section, along PA 233, 0.7 mi south of Colonel Denning State Park, there is a hiker

parking lot on Elk Hill Road. There is parking for about 10 cars.

2. At south end of section there is limited parking at the junction of Cowpens Road and Old Ramp Trail. Cowpens Road is a gravel forest road passable by car. This point can be reached from PA 997 via Three Square Hollow Road, a distance of 4.5 mi.

There is no intermediate road access to this section on roads passable by car. There are several side trails which can be reached from driveable forest roads.

## Maps

    PATC Map J
    USGS 7½' Quadrangles: Andersonburg, Pa.;
       Newville, Pa.; Newburg, Pa.

## Useful Information

**Emergency**-Dial 911

**Services**-Colonel Denning State Park 0.7 mi north on PA 233. Pay phone at park office. Park facilities: Camping, swimming, fishing, nature center and food concession (all seasonal).

## SECTION 3
## NORTH TO SOUTH

| Miles | Detailed Trail Data |
|---|---|
| 0.0 | From the junction of PA 233 and Elk Hill Road in Tuscarora State Forest, proceed west on Elk |

|      | Hill Road. Pass hiker parking lot to right of trail. |
|------|---|
| 0.1  | Pass two cabins along Elk Hill Road. |
| 0.45 | Bear left onto dirt road. |
| 0.5  | Tuscarora State Forest boundary. Leave state forest. |
| 0.6  | Pass *spring* to right of trail then cross small stream. |
| 0.7  | Pass small *spring* to right; pass under powerline. |
| 0.9  | Pass wet weather *spring* on right. |
| 1.0  | Turn right and ascend steeply to an upper forest road. |
| 1.1  | Turn right onto an upper forest road winding up south side of ridge. |
| 1.2  | View to left(southeast) of Cumberland Valley. |
| 1.3  | Enter Tuscarora State Forest, then reach top of ridge. Descend north side of ridge. |
| 1.6  | End of descent. Turn left and begin to reclimb ridge. Blue-blazed trail leads straight ahead a short distance to Meadows Road. |
| 1.8  | Turn right downhill then in 300 ft turn left and continue ascent. |
| 2.1  | Top of ridge. Continue along ridge on old forest road which parallels state forest boundary. |
| 2.5  | Old road to left. |
| 2.6  | Pass property cairn to left of trail. |
| 3.3  | Pipeline clearing with good views to south at top of ridge. |
| 3.6  | Pipeline clearing with views of Bowers Mountain to right(north). |
| 3.9  | Turn left on mountain road (Bill Miller Trail) then in 50 ft turn right. (Trail zigzags along |

| | Blue Mountain ridgetop for next 1.9 mi with several views to south through trees. Small walled *spring* 300 yd north on Bill Miller Trail.) |
|---|---|
| 5.3 | Pass property-corner rock cairn painted orange. Adjacent property boundary is also marked in orange. |
| 5.8 | Cross mountain road (Phoenix Trail). |
| 6.5 | Trail register; please sign in. |
| 7.2 | Turn right and descend slowly from ridgetop. |
| 7.4 | Turn left and proceed southwest with Cowpens Road on right. |
| 7.6 | Cross logging road. |
| 7.8 | Cross logging road. |
| 8.1 | Cross logging road. |
| 8.3 | Turn left away from Cowpens Road. |
| 8.5 | Turn right onto Old Ramp Trail and ascend toward Cowpens Road. |
| 8.6 | Cowpens Road. End of Section 3. Trail continues across Cowpens Road on cleared trail across level top of Blue Mountain. |

## SECTION 3
## SOUTH TO NORTH

| Miles | Detailed Trail Data |
|---|---|
| 0.0 | From Cowpens Road proceed southeast on Old Ramp Trail. |
| 0.1 | Turn left off Old Ramp Trail into woods. |
| 0.3 | Continue with Cowpens Road on left. |
| 0.5 | Cross logging road. |
| 0.8 | Cross logging road. |

| | |
|---|---|
| 1.0 | Cross logging road. |
| 1.2 | Turn right and proceed southeast, climbing to ridgetop. |
| 1.4 | Ridgetop. Turn left and continue on ridgetop. Tuscarora State Forest boundary is just to right of trail. |
| 2.1 | Trail register; please sign in. |
| 2.8 | Cross mountain road (Phoenix Trail). (Trail zigzags along Blue Mountain ridgetop for next 1.9 mi with several views to south through trees. Adjacent property boundary is marked in orange.) |
| 3.3 | Pass property-corner rock cairn painted orange. |
| 4.7 | Turn left on mountain road (Bill Miller Trail) then in 50 ft turn right onto old forest road which parallels state forest boundary. Small walled *spring* 300 yd north on Bill Miller Trail. |
| 5.0 | Pipeline clearing with views of Bowers Mountain to left(north). |
| 5.3 | Pipeline clearing with good views to south at top of ridge. |
| 6.0 | Pass property-corner cairn to right of trail. |
| 6.1 | Old road to right. Continue along ridge on old forest road. |
| 6.5 | Drop off ridgetop to left. |
| 6.8 | Turn right uphill then in 300 ft turn left and continue descent. |
| 7.0 | Turn right and reclimb ridge. Blue-blazed trail to left leads short distance to Meadows Road. |
| 7.3 | Top of ridge. Drop off south side of ridge winding down on an old forest road. Leave Tuscarora State Forest. |

| | |
|---|---|
| 7.4 | View to right(southeast) of Cumberland Valley. |
| 7.5 | Turn left off forest road and descend steeply to a lower forest road. |
| 7.6 | Turn left onto a lower forest road. |
| 7.7 | Pass wet-weather *spring* on left. |
| 7.9 | Pass under powerline, then pass small *spring* to left. |
| 8.0 | Cross small stream then pass *spring* to left of trail. Trail becomes a dirt road. |
| 8.1 | Tuscarora State Forest boundary. Enter state forest. |
| 8.15 | Bear right onto Elk Hill Road. |
| 8.5 | Pass two cabins along Elk Hill Road. |
| 8.6 | Pass hiker parking lot to left of trail. Arrive at PA 233. End of Section 3. Trail turns right(south) along PA 233. |

# Section 4

# AMBERSON RIDGE

Cowpens Road to Hemlock Road
Distance 8.8 miles

**Brief Description of the Section**

This section of the trail is entirely within the Tuscarora State Forest. It crosses and follows many forest roads and trails as well as crossing several ridges. Starting at the junction of Cowpens Road and Old Ramp Trail, at the top of Blue Mountain, the trail enters the woods and soon joins Ramp Road. The trail descends to Laurel Run, then climbs Sherman Mountain (elev. 2180 ft) via switchbacks. After traveling along the ridge it descends again to Second Narrows Road. After crossing another smaller ridge to Sheaffer Run it ascends to Fenton Knob (elev. 2202 ft) on Amberson Ridge, a rise of about 600 ft. After crossing Amberson Ridge it descends steeply about 900 ft to Fowler Hollow Run in Fowler Hollow where it passes a shelter. It then climbs to the top of Rising Mountain (elev. 2020 ft) where it travels along the ridgetop and on a flat below it to Hemlock Road. This last climb is about 700 ft. At the end of the section is the Hemlocks Natural Area, consisting of 131 acres of virgin hemlocks in a narrow ravine about one and one-half miles long. A forest road and trail system in Fowler Hollow leads about 3 mi northeast to Fowlers Hollow State Park. The park has camping facilities and is managed by Colonel Denning State Park. See Section 2 for information on the Tuscarora State Forest and Colonel Denning State Park.

**Parking**

1. At north end of section there is limited parking at the junction of Cowpens Road and Old Ramp Trail. Cowpens Road is a gravel forest road passable by car. This point can be reached from PA 997 via Three Square Hollow Road, a distance of 4.5 mi.

2. At mile 1.9 the trail crosses the North Branch of Three Square Hollow Road. There is limited parking along the edge of road.

3. At mile 3.9 the trail crosses Second Narrows Road. There is limited parking along the edge of the road.

4. At south end of section there is parking for several cars on Hemlock Road at its junction with the trail. This is at the upper end of the Hemlocks Natural Area. This junction is located 4.5 mi southeast of PA 274 at Big Spring State Park. Hemlock Road is a designated snowmobile trail and is closed to vehicle traffic from mid-December to the end of March.

There are several other forest roads which the trail crosses but they are gated and closed to vehicles.

**Maps**

PATC Map J
USGS 7½' Quadrangles: Newburg, Pa.;
    Doylesburg, Pa.

**Useful Information**

**Emergency**-Dial 911
**Services**-Fowlers Hollow State Park 3.0 mi northeast of trail crossing in Fowler Hollow. Park facilities: Pay phone, camping.

## SECTION 4
## NORTH TO SOUTH

| Miles | Detailed Trail Data |
|---|---|
| 0.0 | Junction of Cowpens Road and Old Ramp Trail. Enter woods on trail across from Old Ramp Trail. |
| 0.6 | Turn right onto Ramp Road. |
| 0.7 | Top of ridge. Begin descent of Blue Mountain. |
| 0.9 | Curve left just below top of ridge. |
| 1.1 | Woods road comes in on left. Continue descent. |
| 1.4 | Curve to right on road. |
| 1.6 | Laurel Run; cross stream on footbridge. Continue on Ramp Road. |
| 1.9 | After passing a hunting camp turn left onto Three Square Hollow Road. GNAT hunting camp to right of trail. |
| 2.0 | Turn right off Three Square Hollow Road. |

| | |
|---|---|
| 2.05 | Turn left onto old woods road. |
| 2.3 | Turn right off old woods road. Watch for turns in trail through rocky area. Begin ascent of Sherman Mountain. |
| 2.4 | Ascend steeply on trail with switchbacks. |
| 2.5 | Top of ridge. Turn left(southwest) onto Spotts Road. |
| 2.7 | Site of former Sherman Mountain fire tower. Continue ahead on old woods road (Spotts Trail). |
| 3.2 | Turn right off woods road onto rocky trail. |
| 3.3 | Turn right off ridgetop. Begin steep descent. |
| 3.7 | Descent becomes less steep. |
| 3.85 | Turn right onto woods road (Amberson Valley Trail). |
| 3.9 | Second Narrows Road. Cross road and turn left into swampy area. |
| 4.0 | Pass swampy pond to left of trail and climb small ridge. |
| 4.1 | Cross old woods road. |
| 4.2 | Top of small ridge. Descend into next hollow. |
| 4.5 | Cross Sheaffer Run. |
| 4.55 | Cross lower leg of Couch Road. Begin steep ascent of Amberson Ridge. |
| 4.9 | Turn right onto upper leg of Couch Road. |
| 5.1 | Turn left off road and continue on trail in woods just below top of ridge. |
| 5.3 | Top of ridge. Turn right and begin descent. |
| 5.5 | Enter hemlock forest. Descent becomes very steep. |
| 5.8 | Leave hemlock forest. Continue steep descent. |

| | |
|---|---|
| 5.9 | Turn left onto faint woods road. Descent becomes less steep. |
| 5.95 | Switchback to right off faint woods road. |
| 6.05 | Top of switchback to left on woods road. |
| 6.3 | End of descent. Turn left and cross Fowler Hollow Run on footbridge. Good campsite on east side of stream. |
| 6.4 | Cross forest road. (To right road leads along Fowler Hollow Run to Fowlers Hollow State Park in about 3.0 mi.) |
| 6.5 | Fowlers Hollow Shelter, with covered *spring* to left of trail. This is only shelter on Tuscarora Trail with room for 4 or 5. |
| 6.7 | After passing through wet area with several intermittent *springs* turn left onto an old railroad grade, now Perry Lumber Company Trail. In 100 ft pass a small *spring* and turn right off railroad grade into woods. |
| 6.8 | Turn right and rejoin railroad grade. |
| 6.85 | Bear right off railroad grade and ascend gradually through mostly level forest. |
| 7.1 | Pass small *spring* to right of trail. |
| 7.8 | Base of ridge. Turn right and begin ascent of Rising Mountain. |
| 8.0 | Turn right, ascend on old log skid then turn left. Trail becomes rocky as it zigzags up southeast side of Rising Mountain. |
| 8.3 | Level off just below ridgetop. |
| 8.35 | Ridgetop. Bear left along ridge. |
| 8.4 | Turn right and descend from ridgetop. Soon descend on stone steps. |
| 8.5 | Turn left and roughly parallel Hemlock Road. |

8.8 Junction with Hemlock Road. End of Section 4. Northwest on Hemlock Road it is about 200 ft to *water* and Hemlocks Natural Area (a desirable side trip). Trail proceeds to the left(southwest) onto logging road.

## SECTION 4
## SOUTH TO NORTH

Miles Detailed Trail Data
0.0 Junction with Hemlock Road. (Northwest on Hemlock Road it is about 200 ft to *water* and Hemlocks Natural Area (a desirable side trip). Proceed to right into woods and roughly parallel Hemlock Road.
0.3 Turn right and begin ascent to ridgetop. Soon ascend on stone steps.
0.4 Ridgetop. Bear left along ridge, then continue just below ridgetop.
0.5 Drop off to right, slabbing down southeast side of Rising Mountain. Trail becomes rocky as it zigzags down ridge.
0.8 Turn right, descend on old log skid then turn left.
1.0 Base of ridge. Turn left and continue through mostly level forest.
1.7 Pass small *spring* to left of trail.
1.95 Bear left onto old railroad grade, now Perry Lumber Company Trail.
2.0 Turn left off railroad grade into woods.

| | |
|---|---|
| 2.1 | Rejoin railroad grade and pass small *spring*. In 100 ft turn right off railroad grade and descend through wet area with several intermittent *springs*. |
| 2.3 | Pass covered *spring* to right of trail then arrive at Fowlers Hollow Shelter. This is only shelter on Tuscarora Trail with room for 4 or 5. |
| 2.4 | Cross forest road. (To left road leads along Fowler Hollow Run to Fowlers Hollow State Park in about 3.0 mi.) Descend to stream on woods road. |
| 2.5 | Turn right and cross Fowler Hollow Run on footbridge. Begin long steep ascent of Amberson Ridge. Good campsite on east side of stream. |
| 2.7 | Switchback to left onto old woods road. |
| 2.85 | Switchback to left onto faint woods road. |
| 2.9 | Turn right off faint woods road and begin very steep ascent. |
| 3.0 | Enter hemlock forest. |
| 3.3 | Leave hemlocks. Ascent becomes less steep. |
| 3.5 | Ridgetop. Turn left and continue in woods just below top of Amberson Ridge. |
| 3.7 | Couch Road (upper leg). Turn right and descend on road. |
| 3.9 | Turn left off road and descend steeply. |
| 4.25 | Cross lower leg of Couch Road, and level off. |
| 4.3 | Cross Sheaffer Run and climb small ridge. |
| 4.6 | Top of small ridge. Descend into next hollow. |
| 4.7 | Cross old woods road. |
| 4.8 | Pass swampy pond to right of trail. Pass through swampy area. |

| | |
|---|---|
| 4.9 | Second Narrows Road. Turn right, cross road and continue on woods road (Amberson Valley Trail). |
| 4.95 | Turn left off Amberson Valley Trail onto another woods road and begin ascent of Sherman Mountain. |
| 5.1 | Ascent becomes steeper. |
| 5.5 | Top of ridge. Turn left on rocky trail. |
| 5.6 | Bear left onto old woods road (Spotts Trail). |
| 6.1 | Site of former Sherman Mountain fire tower. Continue ahead on Spotts Road. |
| 6.3 | Turn right(southeast) off Spotts Road and descend steeply on trail with switchbacks. |
| 6.4 | Descent becomes less steep. Watch for turns in trail through rocky area. |
| 6.5 | Turn left onto old woods road. |
| 6.75 | Turn right off woods road. |
| 6.8 | Turn left at Three Square Hollow Road. |
| 6.9 | Turn right off Three Square Hollow Road. GNAT hunting camp to left of trail. Enter woods on old woods road (Ramp Road) and shortly pass another hunting camp. |
| 7.2 | Laurel Run; cross stream on footbridge. Continue on Ramp Road and begin climb of Blue Mountain. |
| 7.4 | Curve to left on road. |
| 7.7 | Woods road comes in on right. Continue ascent. |
| 7.9 | Curve right just below top of ridge. |
| 8.1 | Top of ridge. |
| 8.2 | Turn left off Ramp Road onto trail. |

8.8 Cowpens Road and Old Ramp Trail. End of Section 4. Cross road; trail continues on Old Ramp Trail.

*Mountin laurel*

# Section 5

# KNOB MOUNTAIN

Hemlock Road to PA 641
Distance 11.6 miles

**Brief Description of the Section**

This section of the trail proceeds along the top of Rising Mountain and Knob Mountain for 10.8 mi. At the beginning of this section is the Hemlocks Natural Area consisting of 131 acres of virgin hemlocks in a narrow ravine about one and one-half miles long. Starting at Hemlock Road (elev. 1943 ft) the trail heads southwest along logging roads. Shortly after passing the Stewart Narrows Trail the trail climbs to the crest of Rising Mountain. The trail continues along the rocky crest of Rising Mountain to a high point of 2300 ft. At the end of Rising Mountain, the trail intersects Mountain Road and Catholic Path (elev. 2000 ft). Catholic Path was cut across Rising Mountain as a route for the Catholics living in Amberson Valley to reach the Catholic Church in Doylesburg. The trail continues southwest on Knob Mountain crossing several rocky peaks with many views to the southeast. The trail steeply descends the end of Knob Mountain (elev. 1500 ft) to PA 641, a descent of 700 ft. Carry sufficient water as there is no water in this section. There is a significant problem with blowdowns due to tree mortality caused by gypsy moth defoliation. The northern part of the section is in Tuscarora State Forest while the rest crosses private property. See Section 2 for information on the Tuscarora State Forest.

## Parking

1. At north end of section there is parking for several cars on Hemlock Road at its junction with the trail. This is at the upper end of the Hemlocks Natural Area. This junction is located 4.5 mi southeast of PA 274 at Big Spring State Park. Hemlock Road is a designated snowmobile trail and is closed to vehicle traffic from mid-December to the end of March.

2. At south end of section the trail is at PA 641. There is parking available a short distance south on PA 641 at a roadside shale pit.

There is no intermediate road access to the trail in this section. The only exception is the point where the trail intersects Mountain Road. This road is open, with the owner's permission, from PA 75 in Doylesburg to the top of Rising Mountain. The road is passable by 4-wheel drive when open.

## Maps

PATC Map J
USGS 7½' Quadrangles: Doylesburg, Pa.; Shade Gap, Pa.

## Useful Information

**Emergency**-Dial 911

**Services**-Village of Spring Run is 0.8 mi north on PA 641 at its junction with PA 75. There is a grocery store, restaurant, and gas station with pay phone.

## SECTION 5
## NORTH TO SOUTH

| Miles | Detailed Trail Data |
|---|---|
| 0.0 | Junction with Hemlock Road. (Northeast on Hemlock Road it is about 200 ft to *water* and a trail through the Hemlocks Natural Area containing a stand of virgin hemlocks, a desirable side trip. This is only water until end of section. Road continues on to Big Spring State Park and PA 274 in 4.5 mi.) Proceed uphill(southwest) on logging road. Pass through area of recent logging. |
| 0.6 | Cross Perry/Franklin County line and then pass logging road on left. |
| 0.8 | Turn left off logging road, onto overgrown road through cleared area. |
| 0.9 | At sign pass Stewart Narrows Trail leading left(southeast) 2.3 mi to join Catholic Path. Continue ahead through cleared area. |
| 1.1 | Turn right and climb steeply up last pitch of Rising Mountain. |
| 1.2 | Turn left at top of ridge. |

| | |
|---|---|
| 1.4 | Bear Pond Trail on right leads 1.4 mi back to Hemlock Road. Cross old woods road then ascend to ridge crest. (Trail zigzags along ridgetop crossing several small peaks for next 9.4 mi. Many sections are very rocky but there are also many views.) |
| 2.6 | Rocky outcrop to left of trail. |
| 2.65 | Turn left. After short ascent turn right along ridge crest. |
| 2.7 | Cross open rock field with view to left(southeast). |
| 3.3 | Turn right and descend west side of ridge then turn left and pass through gap between peaks. |
| 3.6 | Bottom of gap. Start climb out of gap. |
| 3.7 | Top of ridge. |
| 3.95 | View to left of trail. |
| 4.0 | View of Kittatinny Mountain and Blue Mountain about 20 yd to left of trail. |
| 4.9 | Turn left. Cross ridge then turn right along east side of ridge. |
| 5.2 | Junction of Mountain Road, Catholic Path and Tuscarora Trail. (Mountain Road leads northwest to town of Doylesburg. Catholic Path leads northeast 1.8 mi and joins Stewart Narrows Trail.) Continue southwest along rough and rocky ridgetop of Knob Mountain. |
| 5.25 | Trail register; please sign in. |
| 5.7 | Cross over very rocky and brushy knife edge for next 0.4 mi. |
| 5.8 | View to left(southeast). |
| 5.9 | Climb steeply to top of rocky peak. |

| | |
|---|---|
| 6.0 | View including PA Turnpike tunnel through Kittatinny Mountain. Knob Mountain drops off very steeply to left(southeast). |
| 6.05 | Cross smooth slab rock (slippery when wet) and drop down through boulders. |
| 6.1 | View of Tuscarora Mountain to right(north). |
| 6.2 | Corner marker of Tuscarora State Forest boundary. Trail zigzags along boundary with state forest on east side of ridge. |
| 6.9 | Jog to left; descend then turn right. |
| 7.4 | Corner marker of Tuscarora State Forest boundary. Continue on ridgetop leaving state forest. |
| 7.6 | Short section of old stone wall to right of trail. Trail is on faint woods road. |
| 7.9 | Pass woods road on right. |
| 8.8 | Junction with Newbridge-Dry Run Road. (Road is open to the west to a farm, emergency use only. Continue on road to ridgetop.) |
| 8.85 | Turn left down east side of ridge. Leave road, enter woods and follow ridgetop. |
| 9.9 | Turn right then left onto an old jeep road which ends at ridgetop. |
| 10.5 | Double powerline with good views in both directions. Cross and continue along ridge. |
| 10.55 | Cross old woods road. |
| 10.8 | Turn right off ridge and descend steeply. |
| 11.1 | At old woods road, continue descent less steeply. |
| 11.2 | Turn left with road and descend through hollow. |
| 11.4 | Turn left off road. Shortly turn right onto another road. |

| | |
|---|---|
| 11.5 | Pass through a shale pit and continue on gravel road. Possible water from *spring* seeps. |
| 11.6 | PA 641. End of Section 5. Village of Spring Run is 0.8 mi north on PA 641. Trail bears left(south) and proceeds along edge of highway. |

## SECTION 5
## SOUTH TO NORTH

| Miles | Detailed Trail Data |
|---|---|
| 0.0 | From PA 641 turn right(east) onto gravel road. (Village of Spring Run is 0.8 mi north on PA 641.) |
| 0.1 | Pass through shale pit on gravel road. Possible water from *spring* seeps. This is only possible water until end of section. Soon begin ascent of Knob Mountain. |
| 0.2 | Turn left off road. Shortly turn right onto another road and ascend through a hollow. |
| 0.4 | Turn right with woods road and continue ascent. |
| 0.5 | Woods road ends. Ascend steeply. |
| 0.8 | Top of ridge; turn left. (Trail zigzags along ridgetop crossing several small peaks for the next 9.4 mi. Many sections are very rocky but there are also many views.) |
| 1.05 | Cross old woods road. |
| 1.1 | Double powerline with good views in both directions. Cross and continue along ridge. |
| 1.7 | Join old jeep road going downhill. Shortly turn right then left along ridge crest. |

| | |
|---|---|
| 2.75 | Intersect Newbridge-Dry Run Road. Follow road down west side of ridge. |
| 2.8 | Leave Newbridge-Dry Run Road. (Road is open to west to farm; emergency use only. |
| 3.7 | Pass woods road on left. |
| 4.0 | Short section of old stone wall to left of trail. Trail is on faint woods road. |
| 4.2 | Corner marker of Tuscarora State Forest boundary. Enter state forest and continue on ridgetop. Zigzag along boundary with state forest on east side of ridge. |
| 4.7 | Jog to left; ascend then turn right. |
| 5.4 | Corner marker of Tuscarora State Forest boundary. State forest on both sides of trail. |
| 5.5 | View of Tuscarora Mountain to left(north). Trail crosses over very rocky and brushy knife edge for next 0.4 mi. |
| 5.55 | Climb through boulders then cross smooth slab rock (slippery when wet). |
| 5.6 | View including PA Turnpike tunnel through Kittatinny Mountain. Knob Mountain drops off very steeply to right(southeast). |
| 5.8 | View to right(southeast). |
| 6.35 | Trail register; please sign in. |
| 6.4 | Junction of Mountain Road, Catholic Path and Tuscarora Trail. (Mountain Road leads northwest to the town of Doylesburg. Catholic Path leads northeast 1.8 mi and joins Stewart Narrows Trail.) Continue northeast along ridgetop of Rising Mountain. |
| 6.7 | Turn left, cross ridge, then turn right along west side of ridge. |

| | |
|---|---|
| 7.6 | View of Kittatinny Mountain and Blue Mountain about 20 yd to right of trail. |
| 7.65 | View to right of trail. |
| 7.9 | Descend into gap between peaks. |
| 8.0 | Bottom of gap. |
| 8.3 | Turn right and ascend west side of ridge then turn left. |
| 8.9 | Cross open rock field with view to right (southeast). |
| 8.95 | Turn left. After short descent turn right below ridge crest. |
| 9.0 | Rocky outcrop to right of trail. |
| 10.2 | Cross old woods road then pass Bear Pond Trail on left, leading 1.4 mi to Hemlock Road. |
| 10.4 | Turn right off ridgetop and descend east side of Rising Mountain. |
| 10.5 | Turn left onto overgrown road through cleared area. |
| 10.7 | Stewart Narrows Trail comes in on right at sign. (Stewart Narrows Trail leads 2.3 mi southeast to join Catholic Path.) Continue ahead through cleared area. |
| 10.8 | Trail intersects logging road. Continue straight ahead on logging road passing through area of recent logging. |
| 11.0 | Pass logging road on right; cross Perry/Franklin County line. |
| 11.6 | Junction with Hemlock Road. End of Section 5. Northeast on Hemlock Road it is about 200 ft to *water* and a trail through the Hemlocks Natural Area containing a stand of virgin hemlocks (a desirable side trip). The road continues on to |

Big Springs State Park and PA 274 in 4.5 mi. Trail proceeds to right and roughly parallels Hemlock Road.

*Path Valley as seen from Big Mountain*

*Cowans Gap Lake*

# Section 6
# COWANS GAP

PA 641 to Cowans Gap State Park
Distance 15.8 miles

**Brief Description of Section**

This section is named for the gap on Tuscarora Mountain at the south end of the section. This gap is named for Samuel Cowan who settled in the area around the time of the American Revolution. From PA 641 the trail follows paved roads crossing PA 75 (elev. 810 ft) in Path Valley. Path Valley was used as part of the route of Tuscarora Indians on their journey north. The trail follows paved Mountain Green Road, then ascends to the crest of Tuscarora Mountain (elev. 1900 ft) on a jeep road passing the Mountain Green Hunting Club. This is a climb of about 1100 ft over 3.9 mi. The trail follows the ridgetop, with several good views and soon enters the Buchanan State Forest. After passing two towers above the Pennsylvania Turnpike, it continues along the ridge until it descends to Fannettsburg-Burnt Cabins Road. The trail continues to descend and follows the South Branch of Aughwick Creek in Allens Valley. The trail uses and crosses many side trails, including Forbes Road Trail, until it reaches Cowans Gap State Park. Forbes Road was the first westward road built through this section of Pennsylvania. It was built to transport and supply troops during the French and Indian wars. Opened in 1755 it was named for and used by General Forbes in 1758.

For information on the Buchanan State Forest or to obtain a public use map contact the forest at the following address:

Buchanan State Forest
R.R. #2, Box 3
McConnellsburg, PA 17233
(717) 485-3148

For information on Cowans Gap State Park or to obtain a Park Recreation Guide contact the park at the following address:

Cowans Gap State Park
HC 17266
Fort Loudon, PA 17224
(717) 485-3948

**Parking**

1. The north end of the section begins at PA 641, 0.8 mi south of the village of Spring Run. There is parking available a short distance south on PA 641 at a roadside shale pit.

2. The trail crosses PA 75, 0.75 mi southwest of the village of Spring Run. There is limited parking along the shoulder of PA 75.

3. The trail meets and uses Mountain Green Road southwest of the village of Spring Run. There is limited parking at the old church just off Mountain Green Road.

Do not park at or block the gate to the Mountain Green Hunt Club.

4. About the midpoint the trail crosses Fannettsburg-Burnt Cabins Road. This road connects with US 522 at Burnt Cabins and with PA 75 at Fannettsburg. There is parking for two or three cars at the trail crossing.

5. About 2.5 mi north of Cowans Gap State Park the trail intersects Allens Valley Road just north of the bridge over Aughwick Creek. There is parking for several cars near the bridge along a wide shoulder area.

6. At south end of section the trail arrives at the junction of Allens Valley, Aughwick and Richmond roads in Cowans Gap State Park. To reach this from US 522 at Burnt Cabins, go south on Allens Valley Road, a distance of approximately 8 mi; from US 30 on Tuscarora Summit go north on Aughwick Road approximately 6.7 mi; and from PA 75 at Richmond Furnace go north on Richmond Road about 4.0 mi. There is ample parking at Cowans Gap State Park. Please check in with park office 0.1 mi south of this road junction for overnight parking.

## Maps

PATC Map K
USGS 7½' Quadrangles: Shade Gap, Pa.; Fannettsburg, Pa.; Burnt Cabins, Pa.

## Useful Information

**Emergency**-Dial 911

**Services**-Village of Spring Run is 0.8 mi north on PA 641 at its junction with PA 75. There is a grocery store, restaurant, and gas station with pay phone.

Village of Fannettsburg, is 2.3 mi east of the trail at the junction of Fannettsburg-Burnt Cabins Road and PA 75. There is a store, P.O. and motel in town.

Cowans Gap State Park has a pay phone at park office. Park facilities: Camping, swimming, fishing, boating and food concession (all seasonal).


## SECTION 6
## NORTH TO SOUTH

| Miles | Detailed Trail Data |
|---|---|
| 0.0 | Trail arrives from northeast on gravel road at PA 641. (Village of Spring Run is 0.8 mi north on PA 641.) Turn left(south) and proceed along edge of highway. |
| 0.3 | Turn right onto Shearer Road. |
| 0.6 | Cross Dry Run on one lane bridge. Bear left up a slight rise, then right away from stream, still following road. |
| 1.0 | Turn right onto PA 75. |
| 1.2 | Turn left off PA 75 onto unpaved farm road. Jog right behind natural gas storage tanks. (Village of Spring Run is 0.75 mi north on PA 75.) |
| 1.5 | Pass farm house on left. Continue straight ahead on farm road, passing lumber yard on left. (Farm is owned by Samuel S. Stoltzfus. He is Amish and very friendly.) |

| | |
|---|---|
| 1.6 | Pass lane on left, leading back into lumber yard. |
| 1.7 | Reach paved Mountain Green Road and turn left. |
| 1.9 | Pass stone ruins to right of road. |
| 2.1 | Pass driveway of first house on Mountain Green Road on left. |
| 2.5 | Pass dairy farm on left. |
| 2.9 | Stony Road comes in from left. |
| 3.4 | Bear left in front of church. |
| 3.5 | Turn right onto unnamed road. |
| 3.6 | Road pavement ends. Pass metal gate. |
| 3.9 | Pass "Mt Green Hunting Club" house on right. Begin ascent of Tuscarora Mountain on dirt jeep road. |
| 4.7 | Pass under powerline just below Tuscarora Mountain crest. |
| 4.8 | After crossing ridge crest, turn left off jeep road and ascend, reaching ridge crest in 0.1 mi. Trail is rough and rocky with many views over the next 3 mi. |
| 5.0 | Pass through pleasant level area. |
| 5.2 | Very nice view on right(west) of valley and mountains. |
| 5.3 | View to right(west). |
| 5.5 | Pass stone property corner. |
| 5.7 | Intersect logging road. Turn left and follow logging road about 100 ft, then turn left onto trail. |
| 5.8 | Pass east side of small peak then pass through small clearcut area. |
| 6.1 | Corner of Buchanan State Forest. Follow forest boundary on left. |

| | |
|---|---|
| 6.75 | Bear left onto tower road. Follow road to towers, then leave road and go right around towers. |
| 6.8 | Lookout tower and microwave tower above Pennsylvania Turnpike tunnel. Lookout tower inaccessible and enclosed by barbed wire. Continue south along ridge. |
| 7.4 | Reach high point of ridge, 1960 ft. |
| 7.9 | Views to east then to west. Better footway begins. |
| 8.0 | View to left(east). |
| 8.4 | Pass TV antennas to left of trail, then pass under pole line. (Good views in both directions. PA Turnpike visible to right, west. More views to left, east, along this section in next 0.7 mi.) |
| 9.05 | Bear right onto jeep road. |
| 9.1 | Fannettsburg-Burnt Cabins Road. Turn right, then left up embankment on opposite side of road. |
| 9.2 | Turn left onto jeep road. |
| 9.5 | Bear right onto old powerline clearing. |
| 9.6 | Cross jeep road and continue on old powerline clearing. |
| 9.7 | Turn left onto woods road. |
| 10.2 | Cross stream. |
| 10.3 | Boundary of Buchanan State Forest. Small stream just ahead. |
| 11.0 | Cross Ellisic Trail just past stream. |
| 11.1 | After short ascent, join newer logging road coming in from left. Continue straight ahead. |
| 11.7 | Junction with Allen Trail which comes downhill from left. Continue ahead on Allen Trail. |

| | |
|---|---|
| 11.8 | Turn right off of logging road and continue to follow Allen Trail. (Orange-blazed high water trail continues 1.2 mi ahead on logging road to Allens Valley Road where it rejoins Tuscarora Trail at mile 12.9.) |
| 11.9 | Cross south branch of Aughwick Creek on bridge. |
| 12.0 | Reach Allens Valley Road. Bear left across paved road and continue on Cove Trail. |
| 12.05 | Turn left on Forbes Road Trail. Link Trail comes in from right. (Orange-blazed Link Trail goes generally north and northwest to connect with Greenwood Spur of Mid-State Trail in Greenwood Furnace State Park, a distance of approximately 65 mi.) |
| 12.1 | *Spring* to right of trail. |
| 12.6 | Piped *spring* to right of trail just past hunting camp. |
| 12.8 | Cross Sharpe Trail, then pass road to hunting camp on right. |
| 12.9 | Reach Allens Valley Road, then turn right onto gated woods road. Orange-blazed high water trail rejoins Tuscarora Trail. |
| 13.4 | Pass woods road going uphill on right. |
| 13.8 | Cross Fox Trail. |
| 14.1 | Small *spring* above trail. Good campsite here and also at clearing just ahead. |
| 14.2 | Cross Wagner Trail. |
| 15.1 | Cross Horseshoe Trail at Cowans Gap State Park boundary. Enter state park. |
| 15.2 | Camping area of Cowans Gap State Park on right. |

| | |
|---|---|
| 15.3 | Turn left off Forbes Road Trail and cross spillway on footbridge. Continue across top of dam, then follow path along edge of lake. |
| 15.6 | Turn left uphill into parking lot #1. Reach paved Allens Valley Road (signed as Aughwick Road) and bear right along road. |
| 15.8 | Junction of Allens Valley, Aughwick and Richmond roads in Cowans Gap State Park. End of Section 6. Park office is a short distance south off Aughwick Road. |

## SECTION 6
## SOUTH TO NORTH

| Miles | Detailed Trail Data |
|---|---|
| 0.0 | Junction of Allens Valley, Aughwick and Richmond roads in Cowans Gap State Park. (Park office is a short distance south off Aughwick Road.) Proceed north on Allens Valley Road. |
| 0.2 | Bear left off Allens Valley Road and pass through parking lot #1. Turn right onto path along edge of lake; continue across top of dam. |
| 0.5 | After crossing spillway on footbridge, turn right onto Forbes Road Trail. |
| 0.6 | Leave camping area of Cowans Gap State Park. |
| 0.7 | Cross Horseshoe Trail at Cowans Gap State Park boundary. Enter Buchanan State Forest. |
| 1.6 | Cross Wagner Trail. |
| 1.7 | Small *spring* above trail. Good campsite. |
| 2.0 | Cross Fox Trail. |
| 2.4 | Pass woods road going uphill on left. |

| | |
|---|---|
| 2.9 | Reach Allens Valley Road, then turn left onto gravel road. (Orange-blazed high water trail goes right on Allens Valley Road, then turns left onto logging road for 1.2 mi where it rejoins Tuscarora Trail at mile 4.0.) |
| 3.0 | Pass road to hunting camp on left, then cross Sharpe Trail. |
| 3.2 | Piped *spring* on left just before hunting camp. |
| 3.7 | *Spring* to left of trail. |
| 3.75 | Turn right off Forbes Road Trail onto Cove Trail. (Link Trail, following Forbes Road, goes straight ahead. Orange-blazed Link Trail goes generally north and northwest to connect with Greenwood Spur of Mid-State Trail in Greenwood Furnace State Park, a distance of approximately 65 mi.) |
| 3.8 | Allens Valley Road. Bear left across paved road and continue on Allen Trail. |
| 3.9 | Cross south branch of Aughwick Creek on bridge. |
| 4.0 | Turn left onto logging road. Orange-blazed high water trail rejoins Tuscarora Trail. |
| 4.1 | Allen Trail turns right uphill. Continue straight |
| 4.7 | Turn left off logging road. Descend. |
| 4.8 | Cross Ellisic Trail just before stream. |
| 5.5 | Cross small stream, then cross boundary of Buchanan State Forest. Leave state forest. |
| 5.6 | Cross stream. |
| 6.1 | Turn right off woods road onto old powerline clearing. Begin ascent. |
| 6.2 | Cross jeep road and continue on old powerline clearing. |

| | |
|---|---|
| 6.3 | Turn left off old powerline clearing onto jeep road. |
| 6.6 | Turn right off jeep road; ascend on rocky trail. |
| 6.7 | Fannettsburg-Burnt Cabins Road. Descend embankment and cross road. Turn right, then left onto a jeep road. |
| 6.75 | Bear left off jeep road. Follow boundary of Buchanan State Forest on right. Several views to right(east) in next 0.7 mi. |
| 7.4 | Pass under pole line. Good views in both directions. PA Turnpike visible to left(west). Pass TV antennas to right of trail. |
| 7.8 | View to right(east). |
| 7.9 | Views to west then to east. Trail is rough and rocky with many views over next 3.0 mi. |
| 8.4 | Reach high point of ridge, 1960 ft. |
| 9.0 | Lookout tower and microwave tower above PA Turnpike. Lookout tower inaccessible and enclosed by barbed wire. Go left around fence then follow tower road briefly. |
| 9.05 | Bear right off tower road onto trail. |
| 9.7 | Corner of Buchanan State Forest. Leave state forest. |
| 10.0 | Pass through small clearcut then pass to east of small peak. |
| 10.1 | Intersect logging road. Turn right, follow logging road about 100 ft then turn right onto trail. |
| 10.3 | Pass stone property corner. |
| 10.5 | View to left(west). |
| 10.6 | Very nice view on left(west) of valley and mountains. |
| 10.8 | Pass through pleasant level area. |

| | |
|---|---|
| 10.9 | Turn left and descend from ridgetop, then turn right onto jeep road. Cross ridge and descend east side of ridge. |
| 11.1 | Pass under powerline just below Tuscarora Mountain crest. |
| 11.9 | Pass "Mt Green Hunting Club" house on left. |
| 12.2 | Pass metal gate. Road pavement begins. |
| 12.3 | Turn left onto Mountain Green Road. |
| 12.4 | Bear right in front of church. |
| 12.9 | Stony Road comes in from right. |
| 13.3 | Pass dairy farm on right. |
| 13.7 | Pass driveway of last house on Mountain Green Road on right. |
| 13.9 | Pass stone ruins to left of road. |
| 14.1 | Turn right off Mountain Green Road onto farm road. (Farm is owned by Samuel S. Stoltzfus. He is Amish and very friendly.) |
| 14.2 | Turn left at fork in farm road and pass lumber yard on right. |
| 14.3 | Pass farm house on right. Continue straight ahead on farm road. |
| 14.6 | Pass natural gas storage tanks then turn right onto PA 75. Village of Spring Run is 0.75 mi north on PA 75. |
| 14.8 | Turn left off PA 75 onto Shearer Road. |
| 15.2 | Cross Dry Run on one lane bridge. |
| 15.5 | PA 641; turn left. |
| 15.8 | At gravel road turn right off PA 641. End of Section 6. The village of Spring Run is 0.8 mi north on PA 641. Trail continues to right(northeast) on gravel road. |

*Hang glider site on Tuscarora Mountain*

## Section 7

# TUSCARORA SUMMIT

Cowans Gap State Park to PA 16
Distance 8.7 miles

**Brief Description of Section**

Most of this section is in the Buchanan State Forest and follows the ridge of Tuscarora Mountain. From Cowans Gap State Park (elev. 1200 ft) the trail climbs steeply to the top of Tuscarora Mountain (elev. 1940 ft), an ascent of 600 ft in 0.8 mi. The trail continues along the ridgetop finally climbing steeply to the top of Big Mountain (elev. 2458 ft), site of a former fire tower. Total ascent has been 1200 ft over a distance of 4.0 mi. The trail continues south on Tuscarora Mountain following a gravel forest road and then Aughwick Road until descending to US 30 at Tuscarora Summit (elev. 2118 ft). After passing Tuscarora Summit Inn the trail passes a hang glider site and a private horse farm before reentering Buchanan State Forest and gradually descending to PA 16 (elev. 1949 ft). About 3.0 mi east on PA 16 is Buchanan Birthplace State Park near the village of Cove Gap. This is the birthplace of President James Buchanan, the only chief executive of the United States from Pennsylvania. See Chapter 6 for information on Buchanan State Forest and Cowans Gap State Park.

## Parking

1. The north end of the section begins at the junction of Allens Valley, Aughwick and Richmond roads in Cowans Gap State Park. To reach this point from US 522 at Burnt Cabins, go south on Allens Valley Road, a distance of approximately 8.0 mi; from US 30 on Tuscarora Summit go north on Aughwick Road approximately 6.7 mi; and from PA 75 at Richmond Furnace go north on Richmond Road about 4 mi. There is ample parking at Cowans Gap State Park. Please check in with park office 0.1 mi south of this road junction, for overnight parking.
2. On US 30 at Tuscarora Summit there is some parking off Aughwick Road on north side of US 30. Tuscarora Summit Inn on the south side does not permit parking.
3. At the south end of the section the trail arrives at US 16 about 3.0 mi east of McConnellsburg. There is parking on the south side of the highway just west of the trail crossing.

## Maps

PATC Map K
USGS 7½' Quadrangles: McConnellsburg, Pa.

## Useful Information

**Emergency**-Dial 911
**Services**-Cowans Gap State Park has pay phone at park office. Park facilities: Camping, swimming, fishing, boating and food concession (all seasonal).

Tuscarora Summit Inn, on US 30 at trail crossing, bar/restaurant with pay phone.

Fort Loudon, PA, 4.5 mi east of the trail at the junction of US 30 and PA 75. There are stores, P.O. and restaurants.

McConnellsburg, PA, about 3.0 mi west of trail at junction of PA 16 and US 522. There are stores, P.O. and restaurants.

Cove Gap, PA, about 3.0 mi east of trail on PA 16 there is a restaurant.

## SECTION 7
## NORTH TO SOUTH

Miles   Detailed Trail Data

0.0   Junction of Aughwick, Richmond and Allens Valley roads in Cowans Gap State Park. (About 0.1 mi north is parking and public telephone. Park office is short distance south off Aughwick Road.) Proceed southeast between Richmond Road and Aughwick Road into picnic area.

0.1   Leave picnic area of Cowans Gap State Park.

0.2   Turn right and ascend steeply to top of Tuscarora Mountain.

0.8   Rocky point at top of ridge with views. Continue along rocky ridge.

0.9   Views to left(east).

1.1   Views to left(east).

1.6   Trail becomes woods road at junction with Geyer Trail. Leave Cowans Gap State Park and enter Buchanan State Forest.

| | |
|---|---|
| 2.2 | Pass Log-Slide Trail on right. |
| 2.6 | Reach start of active logging. Continue on logging road. |
| 3.3 | Turn right on forest road; end of active logging. Continue south through recently logged area. Richmond Trail on right across road. |
| 3.6 | Begin steep ascent. |
| 3.8 | Turn left onto dirt road, bend right and shortly turn left off road. Continue ascent of Big Mountain. |
| 4.0 | Pass through grassy area (possible camping) and turn right, passing site of former Tuscarora Fire Tower on top of Big Mountain. Rock outcrop to left has excellent view to east. Cross gravel Tower Road and enter woods. |
| 4.1 | Leave woods and come to Y in road. Ruins of concrete tower in clearing to left. Continue ahead on gravel Tower Road. |
| 4.7 | Cross Fore Trail. |
| 4.9 | Pass logging road on right. |
| 5.2 | Pass woods road on left. |
| 5.5 | Gated paved road and Plank Trail on left lead to FAA Navigational Aid Station. |
| 5.6 | Parking lot on left. |
| 5.8 | Cross Lincoln Trail. |
| 5.9 | Bear left onto paved Aughwick Road. Pass several microwave and radio towers along west side of road. |
| 6.0 | Cross pipeline clearing. |
| 6.3 | Buchanan State Forest boundary. Leave state forest. |
| 6.5 | View to left(east) along pole line and Oak Drive. |

| | |
|---|---|
| 6.6 | Pass AT&T microwave relay blockhouse on right. |
| 6.8 | After passing "second home" development on Aughwick Road arrive at US 30. (Parking off Aughwick Road north of US 30. Tuscarora Summit Inn does not permit parking south of US 30.) Jog left on US 30 and continue south passing between Tuscarora Summit Inn and abandoned cabins. |
| 6.9 | Pass under powerlines. (Cabled road on right leads 50 yd to hang glider platforms. Excellent views to west of valley and McConnellsburg.) |
| 7.0 | Pass house on left and metal horse barn on right. Please stay on trail. Owner keeps horses in pasture on right. Watch for fence across trail. Pass several horse trails on left. |
| 7.2 | Buchanan State Forest boundary. Enter state forest. |
| 7.4 | Leave state forest. |
| 7.5 | Turn left(east). Trail comes in from right. |
| 7.6 | Reenter state forest. After short descent turn right(south), now following along cleared forest boundary on left. |
| 8.3 | Bottom of sag. Possible camping, no water. |
| 8.6 | Cross gas pipeline. Nice view to east over Buck Run and Cove Mountain. |
| 8.62 | Leave state forest. Pass trail on left and climb to top of ridge. |
| 8.7 | PA 16 just east of ridgetop. End of Section 7. 100 yd west on highway is beautiful view to south. Trail turns left on highway for about 40 yd then goes south, crossing road. |

## SECTION 7
## SOUTH TO NORTH

| Miles | Detailed Trail Data |
|---|---|
| 0.0 | PA 16 just east of ridgetop. (100 yd west on highway is beautiful view to south.) Proceed north from highway. In short distance pass trail on right; continue to left. |
| 0.08 | Follow along cleared, Buchanan State Forest boundary on right(east). |
| 0.1 | Cross gas pipeline. Nice view to east over Buck Run and Cove Mountain. Reenter woods at corner of fence. |
| 0.4 | Bottom of sag. Possible camping, no water. Begin short ascent. |
| 1.1 | Turn left(west) and ascend. Cross state forest boundary and enter private property. |
| 1.2 | Turn right(north). Trail comes in from left. |
| 1.3 | Reenter state forest. |
| 1.5 | Leave state forest. Enter private property; owner keeps horses in pasture on left. Watch for fence across trail. Pass several horse trails on right. |
| 1.7 | Pass metal horse barn on left and house on right. Please stay on trail. |
| 1.8 | Cabled road on left leads 50 yd to hang glider platforms. Excellent views to west of valley and McConnellsburg. Pass under powerlines. |
| 1.9 | Pass between Tuscarora Summit Inn and abandoned cabins to arrive at US 30. (Parking off Aughwick Road north of US 30. Tuscarora Summit Inn does not permit parking south of US 30.) Jog left on US 30 and continue north on |

Aughwick Road, passing "second home" development.

| | |
|---|---|
| 2.1 | Pass AT&T microwave relay blockhouse on left. |
| 2.2 | View to right(east) along pole line and Oak Drive. Pass several microwave and radio towers along west side of road. |
| 2.4 | Buchanan State Forest boundary. Enter state forest. |
| 2.7 | Cross pipeline clearing. |
| 2.8 | Bear right onto gravel Tower Road. |
| 2.9 | Cross Lincoln Trail. |
| 3.1 | Parking lot on right. |
| 3.2 | Gated paved road and Plank Trail on right lead to FAA Navigational Aid Station. |
| 3.5 | Pass woods road on right. |
| 3.8 | Pass logging road on left. |
| 4.0 | Cross Fore Trail. |
| 4.6 | Come to Y in road and enter woods between roads. Ruins of concrete tower in clearing to right. |
| 4.7 | Cross gravel road and turn left passing site of former Tuscarora Fire Tower on top of Big Mountain. Rock outcrop to right has excellent view to east. Pass through grassy area (possible camping), enter woods, and begin descent. |
| 4.9 | Turn right onto dirt road, bend left and shortly turn right off road. Pass through recently logged area. |
| 5.4 | Forest road comes in on left. Continue north on road through active logging area. Richmond Trail on left across road. |
| 6.1 | Reach end of logging; continue on woods road. |

| | |
|---|---|
| 6.5 | Pass Log-Slide Trail on left. |
| 7.1 | Woods road ends at junction with Geyer Trail. Shortly leave Buchanan State Forest and enter Cowans Gap State Park. |
| 7.6 | Views to right(east). |
| 7.8 | Views to right(east). |
| 7.9 | Rocky point at end of ridge with views. Begin steep descent. |
| 8.5 | End of descent. Turn left on level trail. |
| 8.6 | Enter picnic area of Cowans Gap State Park. |
| 8.7 | Junction of Aughwick, Richmond and Allens Valley roads in Cowans Gap State Park. End of Section 7. Park office is a short distance south off Aughwick Road. Trail continues north on Allens Valley Road. |

# Section 8

# THE LOCKINGS

PA 16 to PA 456
Distance 14.5 miles

**Brief Description of Section**

This section is named for The Lockings, the junction of Tuscarora Mountain and Dickeys Mountain near the south end of the section. Most of this section passes through State Game Lands #124 where camping is not permitted. From PA 16 (elev. 1949 ft) the trail proceeds south on Tuscarora Mountain for 12.1 mi with little change in elevation. The footway varies from very rocky to good and there are many excellent viewpoints along the way. There is no water on the ridge but water can be found near the bottom of the ridge on the three major side trails. One should note the vegetation transition taking place along the ridgetop. This was initiated by the gypsy moth devastation of the forest. There is an unusual variety of new plant life not often found on a ridgetop. In addition, ravens and porcupines have been spotted on the ridge. From The Lockings (elev. 2020 ft) there are views into Maryland, Virginia and West Virginia. The trail descends from the Lockings to PA 456 (elev. 527 ft). Most of this 1500 ft descent occurs over a distance of 1.5 mi.

## Parking

1. The section begins at US 16 about 3.0 mi east of McConnellsburg. There is parking on the south side of the highway just west of the trail crossing.

2. On the west side of PA 456 just south of PA 16 there is limited parking near the game lands gate. This is the start of the Alice Trail, which meets the Tuscarora Trail at mile 3.0.

3. There is a game lands parking lot off Ward Drive about 1.0 mi south of PA 456. This is the start of the Hells Hill Trail. This trail is not blazed but cleared and flagged to the Tuscarora Trail at mile 6.0.

4. There is a game lands parking lot 0.8 mi west of PA 456 on a dirt road. This road is about 7.0 mi south of PA 16 and about 2.0 mi north of the village of Sylvan. This is the start of the yellow- and blue-blazed trails, which meet the Tuscarora Trail at mile 7.9

5. There is a large game lands parking lot on both sides of the trail along Furnace Road 0.7 mi north of PA 456.

There is no parking at the junction of PA 456 and Furnace Road at the south end of the section.

## Maps

PATC Map K
USGS 7½' Quadrangles: McConnellsburg, Pa.; Mercersburg, Pa.; Big Cove Tannery, Pa.; Cherry Run, Md.-W.Va.-Pa.

## Useful Information

**Emergency**-Dial 911

**Services**-McConnellsburg, PA, about 3.0 mi west of trail at junction of PA 16 and US 522. There are stores, P.O. and restaurants.

Cove Gap, PA, about 3.0 mi east of trail on PA 16, has a restaurant.

## SECTION 8
## NORTH TO SOUTH

Miles  Detailed Trail Data
- 0.0   PA 16 just east of ridgetop. 100 yd west on highway is beautiful view to south. From point where trail comes in from north, go left(east) 40 yd on highway, turn right(south) and climb up steep bank away from road.
- 0.15  Cross logging road. Pass through area of recent logging for next 0.85 mi.
- 0.3   Cross rock ledges. U.S. Geologic Survey marker in rock to right of trail.
- 0.5   Boundary of State Game Lands #124. Zigzag along boundary with game lands to west.
- 0.8   Cross rock ledges with view to right(west) with leaves off. Trail moves along or near ridgetop with several views to right(west) for next 1.3 mi.
- 1.9   Turn right along ridge; faint woods road continues downhill.

| | |
|---|---|
| 2.05 | Corner marker of State Game Lands #124. Game lands on both sides of trail. |
| 2.1 | Reach cross mountain road (Hunter Road). To left(east) road descends to PA 16. Turn right(west) for about 20 yd and then turn left(south) off road. Again there are many views, especially with leaves off, as trail zigzags its way south along ridgetop. |
| 3.05 | Junction with old woods road (Alice Trail) to left. (Alice Trail gradually descends ridge for 1.4 mi to junction of PA 16 and PA 456. Good *spring* at 1.2 mi from top of ridge.) Continue ahead on ridge. |
| 3.1 | Trail register; please sign in. |
| 4.3 | Pass to west and just below large rock outcrop. Good views in all directions from rocks. |
| 4.6 | View to left(east and southeast). Several views to east over next 0.4 mi. |
| 5.1 | Views both east and west from rock crest. |
| 5.2 | Cross open ledges for next 0.1 mi, with views to left(east). |
| 5.8 | Cross open ledges with views to left(east). |
| 6.0 | Side trail (Hells Hill Trail) leads downhill approximately 1.0 mi to Ward Drive off PA 456. *Spring* near bottom of ridge. |
| 6.2 | Rock overhang. Possible shelter but exposed to west. |
| 7.1 | State Game Lands corner marker (rock cairn) 30 yd to right(west) of trail near ridgetop. |
| 7.2 | Ascend to ridgetop and zigzag along game lands boundary. Game lands on east side of ridge. |
| 7.5 | View to right(west) from rock ledges. |

| | |
|---|---|
| 7.9 | Junction with yellow-blazed trail to left. (It descends east slope of ridge to PA 456 in 2.0 mi. Possible *water* source at 0.9 mi and trail joins dirt road passable by car at 1.2 mi. At 0.3 mi a less steep blue-blazed trail descends ridge 1.1 mi and rejoins yellow trail at 1.0 mi from the top.) |
| 8.5 | Pass large white rock outcrop on left. |
| 8.6 | Bend left along east side of ridge and over rocks, than reascend ridgetop in 0.1 mi. |
| 9.3 | View to left(east) then traverse rocky knife edge of ridge. |
| 10.3 | Cross high point with views to east and west. Alternate trail passes around west side of peak. |
| 10.7 | Cross a secondary peak of ridge. |
| 11.0 | Pass State Game Lands boundary cairn to left(east) of trail. Game lands on both sides of trail. |
| 11.3 | View to right(west). The Lockings below where Dickey Mountain and Tuscarora Mountain meet. Trail register; please sign in. |
| 11.4 | Views to right(west and south). |
| 11.5 | Cross open ledges with views to left(east). |
| 12.1 | Turn sharp left and descend east slope of Tuscarora Mountain. |
| 12.6 | Pass through hollow. *Spring* about 50 yd below trail. |
| 12.8 | Turn left(southeast) on jeep road. |
| 12.9 | Meet and follow stream. |
| 13.0 | Cross stream. |
| 13.5 | Pass between two open meadows and cross small stream. Old split rail fence on right. |

| | |
|---|---|
| 13.6 | Junction with improved game lands road passable for cars. Bear right on improved road. |
| 13.7 | Vehicle gate. Turn right(south) on Furnace Road. |
| 13.8 | Game lands parking on both sides of Furnace Road. Also old barn foundation to right. |
| 13.9 | Turn left(east) on Furnace Road. Shortly pass *spring* house 20 yd to right of road. |
| 14.1 | Boundary of State Game Lands #124. Leave game lands. |
| 14.2 | Pass farm road on right. Continue straight ahead. |
| 14.5 | PA 456. End of Section 8. Trail crosses highway and continues straight ahead on Forge Road. |

## SECTION 8
## SOUTH TO NORTH

| Miles | Detailed Trail Data |
|---|---|
| 0.0 | At PA 456 proceed west on Furnace Road. |
| 0.3 | Pass farm road on left. Continue straight ahead. |
| 0.4 | Boundary of State Game Lands #124. Enter game lands. |
| 0.6 | Pass *springhouse* 20 yd to left of road. Turn right(north) continuing on Furnace Road. |
| 0.7 | Pass old barn foundation on left. Parking for game lands on both sides of Furnace Road. |
| 0.8 | Turn left onto improved game lands road passable by cars. Pass vehicle gate. |

| | |
|---|---|
| 0.9 | Bear left off game lands road onto dirt road. Just ahead is old split rail fence on left. |
| 1.0 | Cross small stream then pass between two open meadows. |
| 1.5 | Cross stream. Trail is now on a jeep road. |
| 1.6 | Turn away from stream. |
| 1.7 | Turn right off jeep road and begin ascent of Tuscarora Mountain. |
| 1.9 | Pass through hollow. *Spring* about 50 yd below trail. |
| 2.4 | End of steep ascent. Turn sharp right and continue northward on Tuscarora Mountain. |
| 3.0 | Cross open ledges with views to right(east). |
| 3.1 | Views to left(west and south). |
| 3.2 | View to left(west). "The Lockings" below where Dickey Mountain and Tuscarora Mountain meet. Trail register; please sign in. |
| 3.5 | Pass game lands boundary cairn on right(east) side of trail. Trail zigzags along game lands boundary. Game lands on east side of ridge. |
| 3.8 | Cross secondary peak of ridge. |
| 4.2 | Cross high point with views to east and west. Alternate trail passes around west side of peak. |
| 5.1 | Traverse rocky knife edge of ridge, then pass view to right(east). |
| 5.8 | Bend right along east side of ridge over rocks, then reascend the ridgetop in 0.1 mi. |
| 6.0 | Pass large white rock outcrop on right. |
| 6.6 | Junction with yellow-blazed trail to right. (It descends east slope of ridge to PA 456 in 2.0 mi. Possible *water* source at 0.9 mi and trail joins dirt road passable by car at 1.2 mi. At 0.3 |

mi less steep blue-blazed trail descends ridge 1.1 mi and rejoins yellow-blazed trail at 1.0 mi from top.
- 7.0 View to left(west) from rock ledges.
- 7.3 Descend from ridgetop.
- 7.4 State Game Lands corner marker (rock cairn) 30 yd west of trail near ridgetop. Game lands on both sides of trail.
- 8.3 Rock overhang. Possible shelter but exposed to the west.
- 8.5 Side trail (Hells Hill Trail) leads downhill approximately 1.0 mi to Ward Drive off PA 456. *Spring* near bottom of ridge.
- 8.7 Cross open ledges with views to right(east).
- 9.2 Cross open ledges for next 0.1 mi with views to right(east).
- 9.4 Views both east and west from rock crest.
- 9.5 View to right(east and southeast). Several views to east over next 0.4 mi.
- 10.2 Pass to west and just below large rock outcrop. Good views in all directions from rocks.
- 11.4 Trail register; please sign in.
- 11.45 Junction with old woods road (Alice Trail) to right. (Alice Trail gradually descends ridge 1.4 mi to junction of PA 16 and PA 456. Good *spring* 1.2 mi from top of ridge.) Continue ahead on ridge. Many views, especially with leaves off, as trail zigzags its way north along ridgetop.
- 12.4 Reach cross mountain road (Hunter Road). To right(east) road descends to PA 16. Turn right(east) for about 20 yd and then turn

| | left(north) off road. Trail moves along or near ridgetop with several views to left(west) for next 1.3 mi. |
|---|---|
| 12.45 | Corner marker of State Game Lands. Trail zigzags along game lands boundary with game lands on west side of trail. |
| 12.6 | Turn left along ridge onto faint woods road which comes in from right. |
| 13.5 | Enter area of recent logging to right. Logging continues for next 0.85 mi. |
| 13.7 | Cross rock ledges with view to left(west), when leaves are off. |
| 14.0 | Boundary of State Game Lands. Leave game lands. |
| 14.2 | Cross rock ledges. U.S. Geologic Survey marker in rock to left of trail. |
| 14.35 | Cross logging road. |
| 14.5 | Descend steep bank and arrive at PA 16 just east of ridgetop. End of Section 8. 100 yd west on highway is beautiful view to south. Trail turns left(west) on highway for about 40 yd then goes right(north) crossing road. |

*Tuscarora Mountain from Forge Road*

# Section 9

# LICKING CREEK

PA 456 to C&O Canal
Distance 9.0 miles

**Brief Description of Section**

This section is named for Licking Creek, a tributary of the Potomac River which the trail crosses and roughly follows in Maryland. From PA 456 (elev. 527 ft) the trail follows the dirt Forge Road and fords Little Cove Creek. It then follows a series of paved roads until it turns onto a jeep road. It fords a tributary of Little Cove Creek (elev. 520 ft) then climbs to the top of Coon Ridge (elev. 770 ft) crossing the Mason and Dixon Line. After passing through private hunting lands the trail enters the Indian Springs Wildlife Management Area. After leaving Indian Springs WMA the trail crosses Licking Creek and passes Camp Harding County Park. Camp Harding Park, established in 1974, was named for President Warren Harding who, with friends Thomas Edison, Harvey Firestone and Henry Ford, visited the area in July 1921. The trail passes under I-70 along the banks of Licking Creek then turns northwest and joins the C&O Canal towpath.

## Parking

There is no parking at the junction of PA 456 and Furnace Road at the north end of the section.
1. There is a large game lands parking lot on both sides of the trail along Furnace Road 0.7 mi north of PA 456.
2. There are several small parking areas in the Indian Springs Wildlife Management Area along Kuhn Ridge Road.
3. Camp Harding Park on Pectonville Road approximately 1.0 mi north of US 40.
4. US 40 just west of Licking Creek, possible parking on shoulder of highway.
5. At south end of the section, there is parking at the end of the paved road at the C&O Canal. This road is entered from US 40 at the west end of the Licking Creek Bridge.

## Maps

PATC Map K
USGS 7½' Quadrangles: Cherry Run, Md.-W.Va.-Pa.

## Useful Information

**Emergency**-Dial 911
**Services**-Camp Harding County Park. Open 9:00 am to sunset, May through October; water tap, pay phone, ball fields and picnic shelters.

## SECTION 9
## NORTH TO SOUTH

| Miles | Detailed Trail Data |
|---|---|
| 0.0 | At PA 456 cross highway and proceed on dirt Forge Road. |
| 0.5 | Ford Little Cove Creek. |
| 1.0 | Road junction; pavement begins. Cross small creek on bridge and bear right(south) continuing on Forge Road. |
| 1.2 | Cross gas pipeline. |
| 1.7 | Junction with Little Cove Road. Turn right(west). |
| 1.9 | Turn very sharp left onto jeep road passable by four-wheel drive only. |
| 2.0 | Ford stream. |
| 2.1 | Jog right then left and begin climb to top of Coon Ridge. |
| 2.3 | Bend sharply right on road. |
| 2.4 | Turn left on road. Cross Mason and Dixon Line. |
| 2.5 | Bear left onto Kuhn Ridge Road. Pass hunting camp on right. |
| 3.2 | Boundary of Indian Springs Wildlife Management Area. Continue on Kuhn Ridge Road. |
| 4.8 | Slabtown Road comes in on right. Continue straight ahead on Slabtown Road. |
| 5.0 | Junction of Mooresville, Pectonville and Slabtown roads. Continue south on paved Pectonville Road. |
| 5.2 | Boundary of Indian Springs Wildlife Management Area. Leave area and continue south. |
| 6.0 | Bear right(west) on road along Licking Creek. |

| | |
|---|---|
| 6.2 | Cross bridge over Licking Creek. |
| 6.6 | Junction of Pectonville and Little Galilee roads. Turn left following Pectonville Road east. |
| 6.65 | Camp Harding County Park entrance on left. (Park has phone, picnic area and ball fields for use in season.) Turn right following Pectonville Road. |
| 6.7 | Galilee Road comes in on right. |
| 7.8 | Junction with US 40. Turn left(east) along highway. |
| 8.2 | At Licking Creek bridge, turn right(south) on paved road. |
| 8.3 | Pass under I-70 bridges. |
| 8.4 | Turn right with road and go west away from Licking Creek. |
| 8.5 | Jog left across old Western Maryland RR track bed and continue west on road. |
| 8.95 | Turn left(south) onto dirt road. |
| 9.0 | After passing gate across road arrive at canal towpath. End of Section 9. Trail turns right(west) and continues on canal towpath. |

## SECTION 9
## SOUTH TO NORTH

| Miles | Detailed Trail Data |
|---|---|
| 0.0 | At dirt road junction with canal towpath turn left(north) and proceed on dirt road. |
| 0.05 | After passing gate across road turn right(east) onto paved road. |

| | |
|---|---|
| 0.5 | Jog left across old Western Maryland RR track bed and continue east on road. |
| 0.6 | Turn left with road and go north along Licking Creek which lies to right. |
| 0.7 | Pass under I-70 bridges. |
| 0.8 | Arrive at US 40. Turn left(west) along highway. |
| 1.2 | Pectonville Road. Turn right(north). |
| 2.3 | Galilee Road comes in on left. |
| 2.35 | Camp Hardy County Park entrance on right. (Park has phone, picnic area and ball fields for use in season.) Turn left following Pectonville Road. |
| 2.4 | Junction of Pectonville and Little Galilee roads. Turn right following Pectonville Road north. |
| 2.8 | Cross bridge over Licking Creek. Turn right and follow Licking Creek. |
| 3.0 | Bear left(north) away from creek on road. |
| 3.8 | Boundary of Indian Springs Wildlife Management Area. |
| 4.0 | Junction of Mooresville, Pectonville and Slabtown roads. Continue north on dirt Slabtown Road. |
| 4.2 | Slabtown road goes off to left. Continue straight ahead on Kuhn Ridge Road through Indian Springs Wildlife Management Area. |
| 5.8 | Boundary of Indian Springs Wildlife Management Area. Leave area and continue on dirt road along Coon Ridge. |
| 6.5 | Pass hunting camp on left. Bear right onto another road passable by four-wheel drive only. |
| 6.6 | Turn right on road. Cross Mason and Dixon Line. |

| | |
|---|---|
| 6.7 | Bend sharp left on road. |
| 6.8 | Jog right then left after descending Coon Ridge. |
| 7.0 | Ford stream. |
| 7.1 | Turn very sharp right onto paved Little Cove Road and proceed east. |
| 7.3 | Junction with paved Forge Road. Turn left(north). |
| 7.8 | Cross gas pipeline. |
| 8.0 | Road junction. Bear left(northwest) on Forge Road and cross small creek on bridge. Road pavement ends. |
| 8.5 | Ford Little Cove Creek. |
| 9.0 | PA 456. End of Section 9. Trail crosses highway and continues on dirt Furnace Road. |

*Chesapeake & Ohio Canal*

*Lock 52, C&O Canal and towpath*

# Section 10

# C&O CANAL

Licking Creek to Hancock (MD 144)
Distance 7.9 miles

**Brief Description of Section**

This easy and interesting section is entirely on the C&O Canal towpath. There are two locks, one aqueduct, and a natural depression known as Little Pool with a camping area nearby. The C&O Canal is maintained by the National Park Service and does not allow blazing. Detailed descriptions of this canal and its history are available in several publications. Two of these containing descriptions of the canal section traversed by the Tuscarora Trail are:

*Towpath Guide to the C&O Canal*, Thomas F. Hahn, American Canal and Transportation Center, 809 Rathton Road, York, PA 17403

*184 Miles of Adventure: Hikers' Guide to the C&O Canal*, Mason-Dixon Council, Boy Scouts of America

For information from the National Park Service please write to:

C&O Canal National Historic Park
P.O. Box 4
Sharpsburg, MD 21782

## Parking

1. At north end of the section, there is parking at the end of the paved road at the C&O Canal. This road is entered from US 40 at the west end of the Licking Creek Bridge.
2. At the east end of Hancock, off MD 144, there is an access road to Lock 52 and Little Tonoloway Creek aqueduct. Limited parking.
3. Downtown Hancock, off MD 144 there is a large parking area on Church Street near the Iron Bridge.
4. At south end of section, Little Tonoloway Park. Entrance is at end of Pennsylvania Avenue off MD 144 at west end of town.

## Maps

PATC Map K
USGS 7½' Quadrangles: Cherry Run, Md.-W.Va.-Pa.; Hancock, W.Va.-Md.-Pa.

## Useful Information

**Emergency**-Dial 911
**Services**-Hancock, MD, is a full service town. There is a P.O., several restaurants, stores, and motels. Little Tonoloway Park has a boat ramp and picnic tables, but no camping. There is a Park Service Visitor Center located on MD 144 near the east end of town (301) 678-5463. Path Finders Outfitters is located on Pennsylvania Avenue near the entrance to Little Tonoloway Park, (301) 678-6870. They have bicycle and canoe rentals and

supplies plus some camping supplies. They also offer a shuttle service.

## SECTION 10
## NORTH TO SOUTH

Miles  Detailed Trail Data
0.0    Trail arrives at towpath on dirt road. Turn right and proceed west on towpath. (Licking Creek aqueduct and hiker-biker camping area are 0.6 mi east of this point. No blazes in this section; Park Service ruling.)
3.45   Lower end of Little Pool, a body of water nearly 1.0 mi long and to right of trail.
4.0    Little Pool hiker-biker campground.
4.35   Upper end of Little Pool.
6.2    Canal Lock 51.
6.3    Road across canal leads to MD 144 in 0.1 mi. Shortly pass Canal Lock 52 and Tonoloway Creek aqueduct.
7.5    Town of Hancock.
7.6    Iron bridge to right leads to Church Street. To left is old road and gauging station.
7.9    Entrance road to Little Tonoloway Park on left. End of Section 10. Trail turns right(north) across canal onto Pennsylvania Avenue, which leads to Main St (MD 144).

# SECTION 10
# SOUTH TO NORTH

| Miles | Detailed Trail Data |
|---|---|
| 0.0 | Trail arrives at towpath after crossing canal at end of Pennsylvania Avenue, entrance road to Little Tonoloway Park. Turn left(east) and follow towpath. (No blazes in this section; Park Service ruling.) |
| 0.3 | Iron bridge to left leads to Church Street. To right is old road and gauging station. |
| 0.4 | Town of Hancock. |
| 1.6 | Pass Tonoloway Creek aqueduct and canal Lock 52. Shortly pass road across canal which leads to MD 144 in 0.1 mi. |
| 1.7 | Canal Lock 51. |
| 3.55 | Upper end of Little Pool, body of water nearly 1.0 mile long to left of trail. |
| 3.9 | Little Pool hiker-biker campground. |
| 4.45 | Lower end of Little Pool. |
| 7.9 | Dirt road on left. End of Section 10. Trail turns left(north) from towpath. (Licking Creek aqueduct and hiker-biker camping area is 0.6 mi east of this point.) Blazing resumes. |